HSE
Health & Safety
Executive

A pain in your workplace?

Ergonomic problems and solutions

HSE BOOKS

The Health and Safety Executive gratefully acknowledges the assistance of Hu-Tech Associates and System Concepts Ltd in collecting these case studies.

CONTENTS

Preface   *v*

How to use this book   *vii*

Table of case studies   *viii*

Case studies   *1*

Radio equipment assembly   *3*

Assembly line operation   *4*

Palletisation of vehicle components   *5*

Spot welding body shop assembly   *6*

General duties using a VDU   *8*

Secretarial duties using a VDU   *9*

VDU operation   *11*

Wire harness operation   *12*

Loading produce trays into a delivery van   *13*

Handling patients in a hospital   *14*

Handling infirm patients in a bathroom area   *15*

Baggage handling   *16*

Racking operations in drying room   *18*

Computer disk drive assembly   *19*

Material storage   *20*

Computer hard disk workstation   *21*

Washing utensils in a sink   *22*

Control box assembly   *23*

Packing on a production line   *24*

Telephone exchange equipment assembly   *26*

Spring brake actuator assembly   *27*

Test stand operation   *28*

Aerospace assembly task   *29*

Gear and cover assembly   *31*

Electronics assembly   *32*

Tie bar assembly   *33*

Accountancy secretarial work   *34*

Multi-function printed circuit board assembly   *35*

Preparing wax patterns for engine parts manufacture   *36*

Use of airport check-in desks   *37*

Intensive keyboard use   *38*

Assembly work while standing   *39*

Use of hand tools   *40*

Use of large powered tools   *41*

Cutting denim using a powered cutter   *42*

Work at a supermarket delicatessen counter   *43*

Pneumatic stapling task   *44*

Microscope use in laboratories   *45*

46   *Intensive telephone and keyboard use*

47   *Vehicle trim-cutting*

48   *Nut running operations in engine manufacture*

49   *Manifold assembly*

50   *Removing unwanted threads from jeans*

51   *Nut running operation*

52   *Application of torques*

53   *Clip installation*

54   *Button cluster assembly*

55   *Heart valve construction*

56   *Date-maker sub-assembly operations*

57   *Tyre sequencing*

58   *Replacing coal onto a conveyor belt*

59   *Cased beer distribution*

60   *Packing linen boxes*

61   *Paper tissue winding machine operation*

62   *Fabric roll slitting operation*

63   *Photocopier manufacture*

64   *Games packing operation*

66   *Spring bundling*

67   *Gas cooker 'splashback' assembly*

68   *Component sub-assembly operation*

70   *Legal secretarial work*

71   *Manufacturing jeans*

73   *Actuator remanufacturing*

74   *Coil handling*

75   *Battery replacement on automatic guided vehicles*

76   *Upending whisky casks*

77   *Stillaging cask beer*

78   *Fitting seats into vehicles*

79   *Remanufacture component sorting*

80   *Preparation, weighing and mixing of raw materials*

82   *Gas cooker assembly*

84   *Recovery of shopping trolleys from car parks*

85   *Decanting parts for car assembly*

86   *Folding and stitching material*

88   *Engine manufacture*

89   *Reaming operation*

90   *Sewing hems on jeans*

92   Further publications and sources of advice

94   Acknowledgements

PREFACE

This book is for all employers whose work might be putting their employees' muscles and joints at risk of damage. Backaches, sore shoulders or elbows, or numb or tingling wrists and hands are sometimes due to work. This book describes the causes of these problems and shows simple and cost-effective ways of reducing them. These are 'real life' cases. The solutions were successful answers to actual problems which companies had.

WHO IS AT RISK? Risks of damage to muscles and joints ('musculoskeletal' risks) are not confined to particular industrial sectors or types of people. Often thought of as associated with 'heavy' jobs, they are increasingly found in service industries. Survey information suggests that in 1990 there were nearly 900 000 cases caused or made worse by work.

WHY DO THESE PROBLEMS ARISE? When they are related to work they are often caused by poor workplace or job design. These can mean:
- poor working positions - awkward or static postures;
- high levels of force;
- high levels of repetition;
- difficult manual handling tasks;
- too much bending, stretching or effort.
   The back, neck, shoulders and upper limbs are particularly at risk.

HOW DO WE KNOW IF WE HAVE A PROBLEM? Health problems show up in different ways, such as:
- cases of injury to backs and limbs;
- aches and pains;
- poor product quality;
- high material waste;
- low output;
- frequent employee complaints and rest stops;
- do-it-yourself 'improvements' to workstations and tools (eg seat padding);
- employees wearing bandages, splints, rub-ons, copper bracelets.
   Talk informally to employees. Their comments may suggest you need to assess the risks in more detail. Some of these conditions are chronic and develop slowly. It is very important to catch them early. Make sure you have a system for employees to report problems, aches and pains. Encourage them to do so.

WHY DO WE NEED TO TAKE ACTION?   New Regulations require you to assess health and safety risks to your workers. They are the:
- Management of Health and Safety at Work Regulations 1992;
- Manual Handling Operations Regulations 1992;
- Display Screen Equipment Regulations 1992;
- Provision and Use of Work Equipment Regulations 1992;
- Workplace (Health, Safety and Welfare) Regulations 1992.

On top of this, these problems are probably costing you money, from sickness absence, high staff turnover, retraining, loss of production etc. Compensation cases are increasing, and problems may affect your insurance premium.

Adapting jobs to suit the individuals doing them often reduces fatigue and increases motivation and satisfaction. This leads to increased productivity and better health and well-being, as many of these case studies show.

HOW TO IMPLEMENT SOLUTIONS   The risky features of a job can be removed or reduced through changes to the design of workstations, tools and work organisation. Even simple solutions can have a marked impact and reduce complaints and disorders. Simple solutions are often better - easier to implement and adjust to. You are probably using some already without realising they are preventing damage.

You may have an isolated problem and find in this book a straightforward solution to it. Or you may find a range of problems. HSE publications (see page 92) give guidance on assessing and reducing risks. Arrangements already in place for managing other health and safety risks in your workplace should need only small adaptations to cope with these types of risk. Some helpful principles are:
- You will need to prioritise your activity, for example by tackling serious risks affecting a number of employees before an isolated complaint of minor discomfort.
- It can help to find a few possible solutions. Don't always take the first idea put forward.
- Try solutions ideas out on a small scale and modify them if necessary before you move on to full implementation. What works in one situation may need adapting a little for another - and check your solution has not caused new risks.
- The success of the solutions depends on sensitive management of their implementation. Imposed solutions often don't work.
- Involve employees in identifying and solving the problems, encourage 'ownership' of the solutions and success is more likely. The case studies show that a team approach or task force helps a lot.
- Fit short-term local initiatives into the company's overall health and safety strategy. That way, benefits become long-term.
- Monitor the situation to make sure solutions are still effective at a later date and keep abreast of new technological developments. The solutions you implement now may be superseded by better ideas in months and years to come - but this book can help you now.

HOW TO USE THIS BOOK

Each study describes:

- body area affected;

- risk factors;

- type of solution;

- relevance of the case in other situations.

It is uncommon for just one factor to cause the problem. Repetition, for example, is often only a problem when other risk factors are present. Most of the case studies identify several different risk factors and show how they have been controlled. The body area affected, risk factors and type of solution are summarised at the side of each page to help you identify risks and solutions relevant to your situation. Remember that answers to problems in one industry may work just as well in another. The table starting on page viii sets out a summary of each study to help steer you through the book.

Body area affected

Risk factors

Type of solution

RELEVANCE OF THE CASE IN OTHER SITUATIONS

Body area affected	Risk factors	Type of solution	Case study	Page
shoulder	awkward posture manual handling	workspace organisation	**RADIO EQUIPMENT ASSEMBLY**	3
shoulder	awkward posture	workspace organisation workstation design	**ASSEMBLY LINE OPERATION**	4
upper limb	awkward posture	workspace organisation component design	**PALLETISATION OF VEHICLE COMPONENTS**	5
upper limb back	awkward posture	workspace organisation tool design	**SPOT WELDING BODY SHOP ASSEMBLY**	6
neck	awkward posture	workspace organisation workstation design	**GENERAL DUTIES USING A VDU**	8
neck wrist	awkward posture	workspace organisation workstation design tool design	**SECRETARIAL DUTIES USING A VDU**	9
shoulder arm	awkward posture	workspace organisation	**VDU OPERATION**	11
upper limb	awkward posture	workspace organisation workstation design	**WIRE HARNESS OPERATION**	12
back	awkward posture manual handling	workstation design	**LOADING PRODUCE TRAYS INTO A DELIVERY VAN**	13
back	manual handling awkward posture	workstation design	**HANDLING PATIENTS IN A HOSPITAL**	14
back	manual handling awkward posture	workstation design mechanisation	**HANDLING INFIRM PATIENTS IN A BATHROOM AREA**	15
back	manual handling awkward posture	workstation design	**BAGGAGE HANDLING**	16
knee	awkward posture	workstation design	**RACKING OPERATIONS IN A DRYING ROOM**	18
neck wrist	awkward posture	workstation design	**COMPUTER DISK DRIVE ASSEMBLY**	19
back shoulder	awkward posture	workstation design	**MATERIAL STORAGE**	20
back shoulder	awkward posture	workstation design	**COMPUTER HARD DISK WORKSTATION**	21
shoulder neck back	awkward posture	workstation design	**WASHING UTENSILS IN A SINK**	22

Body area affected	Risk factors	Type of solution	Case study	Page
lower back	awkward posture	workstation design	**CONTROL BOX ASSEMBLY**	23
upper limbs	awkward posture	workstation design task design	**PACKING ON A PRODUCTION LINE**	24
back arm shoulder	awkward posture	workstation design tool design	**TELEPHONE EXCHANGE EQUIPMENT ASSEMBLY**	26
shoulder arm	applied force	workstation design	**SPRING BRAKE ACTUATOR ASSEMBLY**	27
elbow shoulder	repetition applied force awkward posture	workstation design machinery design	**TEST STAND OPERATION**	28
wrist shoulder	grip applied force awkward posture	workstation design tool design	**AEROSPACE ASSEMBLY TASK**	29
upper limb back	awkward posture grip	workstation design machinery design task design	**GEAR AND COVER ASSEMBLY**	31
shoulder neck	awkward posture	workstation design	**ELECTRONICS ASSEMBLY**	32
shoulder	awkward posture grip	workstation design tool design	**TIE BAR ASSEMBLY**	33
upper limb	awkward posture	workstation design	**ACCOUNTANCY SECRETARIAL WORK**	34
upper limb	awkward posture repetition	workstation design tool design component design	**MULTI-FUNCTION PRINTED CIRCUIT BOARD ASSEMBLY**	35
back upper limb	awkward posture	workstation design	**PREPARING WAX PATTERNS FOR ENGINE PARTS MANUFACTURE**	36
neck upper limb	repetition awkward posture	workstation design workspace organisation	**USE OF AIRPORT CHECK-IN DESKS**	37
neck lower back legs	awkward posture	workstation design	**INTENSIVE KEYBOARD USE**	38
lower back legs	awkward posture	workstation design	**ASSEMBLY WORK WHILE STANDING**	39
hand	grip applied force	tool design	**USE OF HAND TOOLS**	40

Body area affected	Risk factors	Type of solution	Case study	Page
hand	grip applied force	tool design	**USE OF LARGE POWERED TOOLS**	41
upper limb	force awkward posture	tool design	**CUTTING DENIM USING A POWERED CUTTER**	42
neck arm shoulder lower back lower legs	awkward posture	tool design task design workstation design	**WORK AT A SUPERMARKET DELICATESSEN COUNTER**	43
shoulder	awkward posture applied force	tool design	**PNEUMATIC STAPLING TASK**	44
shoulder back	awkward posture	tool design	**MICROSCOPE USE IN LABORATORIES**	45
neck shoulder	awkward posture repetition	tool design	**INTENSIVE TELEPHONE AND KEYBOARD USE**	46
hand	grip applied force repetition	tool design individual organisation	**VEHICLE TRIM-CUTTING**	47
shoulder	awkward posture applied force	tool design	**NUT RUNNING OPERATIONS IN ENGINE MANUFACTURE**	48
hand	awkward posture repetition applied force	tool design workstation design	**MANIFOLD ASSEMBLY**	49
upper limb	applied force repetition grip	tool design	**REMOVING UNWANTED THREADS FROM JEANS**	50
elbow upper arm	repetition awkward posture applied force	tool design	**NUT RUNNING OPERATION**	51
elbow back shoulder	applied force	tool design	**APPLICATION OF TORQUES**	52
shoulder upper limb	awkward posture	tool design workstation design	**CLIP INSTALLATION**	53
hand wrist	repetition grip applied force	supporting clamp/jig component selection	**BUTTON CLUSTER ASSEMBLY**	54

Body area affected	Risk factors	Type of solution	Case study	Page
hand	awkward posture grip applied force repetition	supporting clamp/jig task design	**HEART VALVE CONSTRUCTION**	55
upper limb	applied force awkward posture grip	supporting clamp/jig workstation design	**DATE-MAKER SUB-ASSEMBLY OPERATIONS**	56
upper limb back	manual handling	task design workstation design	**TYRE SEQUENCING**	57
back	awkward posture manual handling	task design machinery design	**REPLACING COAL ONTO A CONVEYOR BELT**	58
back	manual handling repetition	task design	**CASED BEER DISTRIBUTION**	59
back upper limb	manual handling	component design	**PACKING LINEN BOXES**	60
elbow back shoulder	manual handling repetition	component design	**PAPER TISSUE WINDING MACHINE OPERATION**	61
hand wrist	applied force repetition	component design	**FABRIC ROLL SLITTING OPERATION**	62
upper limb	awkward posture grip applied force	component design	**PHOTOCOPIER MANUFACTURE**	63
upper limb	awkward posture grip applied force	component design task design workstation design	**GAMES PACKING OPERATION**	64
wrist lower arm	grip applied force repetition	component design tool design	**SPRING BUNDLING**	66
elbow upper arm	awkward posture	component design tool design workstation design	**GAS COOKER 'SPLASHBACK' ASSEMBLY**	67
upper limb	grip applied force awkward posture	component design task design workstation design	**COMPONENT SUB-ASSEMBLY OPERATION**	68
wrist elbow	repetition awkward posture	individual organisation	**LEGAL SECRETARIAL WORK**	70

Body area affected	Risk factors	Type of solution	Case study	Page
upper limb	repetition applied force	individual organisation workstation design	**MANUFACTURING JEANS**	71
shoulder	applied force repetition	machinery design	**ACTUATOR REMANUFACTURING**	73
back shoulder	applied force awkward posture	machinery design	**COIL HANDLING**	74
back	manual handling	mechanisation	**BATTERY REPLACEMENT ON AUTOMATIC GUIDED VEHICLES**	75
back	manual handling awkward posture	mechanisation	**UPENDING WHISKY CASKS**	76
back	manual handling awkward posture	mechanisation	**STILLAGING CASK BEER**	77
back	manual handling awkward posture repetition	mechanisation	**FITTING SEATS INTO VEHICLES**	78
back shoulder	manual handling awkward posture	mechanisation	**REMANUFACTURE COMPONENT SORTING**	79
back	manual handling repetition	mechanisation workstation design	**PREPARATION, WEIGHING AND MIXING OF RAW MATERIALS**	80
back upper limb	manual handling awkward posture	mechanisation tool design workstation design	**GAS COOKER ASSEMBLY**	82
back shoulder upper and lower limb	applied force awkward posture manual handling	mechanisation	**RECOVERY OF SHOPPING TROLLEYS FROM CAR PARKS**	84
upper limb	repetition applied force	mechanisation	**DECANTING PARTS FOR CAR ASSEMBLY**	85
upper limb back	awkward posture applied force repetition	mechanisation individual organisation	**FOLDING AND STITCHING MATERIAL**	86
back upper limb	awkward posture	automation	**ENGINE MANUFACTURE**	88
upper limb back shoulder	awkward posture applied force	automation	**REAMING OPERATION**	89
wrist	applied force repetition awkward posture	automation	**SEWING HEMS ON JEANS**	90

CASE STUDIES

RADIO EQUIPMENT ASSEMBLY

TASK A task assembling secure radio equipment involved lifting and moving a tray containing a heavy piece of radio equipment from one workbench to another several times per hour.

PROBLEM The operative carrying the tray had pain in her shoulders and sought medical advice. She was diagnosed as having a 'frozen' shoulder. She did not take time off work and only reported the problem after the diagnosis.

ASSESSING THE RISKS AND FINDING SOLUTIONS The site health and safety manager watched the operative's posture while she did the task. To move the tray and radio to the second workbench she had to lift the load and twist her upper body. This was thought to be the cause of her pain.

    The safety manager had the two workbenches pushed together so that the operator did not need to lift the radio. She only had to push the tray a short distance from one bench to the other.

    The modification cost nothing.

RESULTS After this simple modification, the user's working posture improved and the pain stopped.

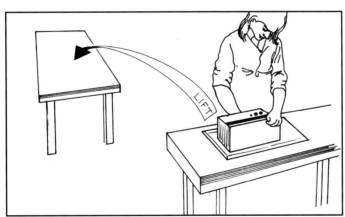

Before

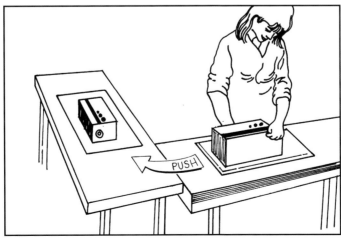

After

Shoulder

Awkward posture
Manual handling

Workspace organisation

IN MANY JOBS WHERE MATERIALS NEED TO BE TRANSPORTED, REMEMBER:
* LIFTING HEAVY WEIGHTS WHILE TWISTING THE UPPER BODY IS LIKELY TO CAUSE UPPER LIMB DISCOMFORT;
* OBSERVING A TASK BEING DONE CAN OFTEN SUGGEST A SOLUTION;
* INDEPENDENT OBSERVATION BY TRAINED HEALTH AND SAFETY PERSONNEL CAN OFTEN LEAD TO A SOLUTION - THE SUFFERER IS SOMETIMES TOO CLOSE TO THE JOB TO SEE A SOLUTION AND MAY BE UNEASY ABOUT SUGGESTING CHANGES;
* OFTEN WITH HANDLING TASKS, THE BEST SOLUTION IS TO REMOVE THE LIFTING;
* WORKSTATION MODIFICATIONS NEED NOT BE COSTLY TO BE EFFECTIVE.

Shoulder

Awkward posture

Workspace organisation
Workstation design

PARTS ASSEMBLY IS REQUIRED IN SEVERAL MANUFACTURING INDUSTRIES. REPOSITIONING THE MAIN COMPONENTS OF THE WORKSTATION CAN GREATLY IMPROVE OPERATORS' UPPER LIMB POSTURE AND OVERALL COMFORT. ANOTHER IMPORTANT PRINCIPLE IS CONSULTATION WITH THE OPERATOR TO IDENTIFY THE PROBLEMS AND DESIGN THE APPROPRIATE SOLUTION.

TASK   In an automative assembly plant a seated operator assembled wire harnesses on a small trolley which ran on a track in front of her. The operation went as follows:

Before

- take a part from a bin to the right of the chair and snap it into place in the partly-assembled unit in the trolley;
- grab a wire part from a second parts bin behind and to the left of the operator. The parts bin was brought to the workstation on a roller conveyor behind the operator;
- mark the wire part using a marking machine in front of the operator;
- press one end of the wire into the unit and wrap the free end into its place;
- press a foot control to cycle the conveyor and bring the next trolley in front of the operator.

Three operators each assembled approximately 100 units per hour.

PROBLEM   One operator had complained to the company nurse of shoulder pain.

ASSESSING THE RISKS AND FINDING SOLUTIONS

Hazard/risk	*Solution*
The position of the second parts bin behind operator meant she had to reach behind each time she wanted a part.	The roller conveyor with the parts bin was repositioned directly on the employee's left side.
Poor posture in general.	The employee was consulted about the position of her chair, and her footrest was adjusted to suit the new chair height.

The modifications cost almost nothing.

RESULTS
- Improved posture when reaching for the second bin.
- No more reports of discomfort.

PALLETISATION OF VEHICLE COMPONENTS

TASK   Small, light components at an assembly workstation are picked out of crates and fitted into vehicles, eg plastic parts of the instrument fascia. The components come into the production area in several different size crates.

PROBLEM   Operators fitting the components were suffering upper limb discomfort.

ASSESSING THE RISKS AND FINDING SOLUTIONS   The operators had to reach into the crates and stretch to take the last few components out. It was more difficult with the smaller components. Although not a high risk activity, the problem was common to many of the component fitting areas in the factory.

   The crates were put into racks at waist and shoulder height that fitted at a 30° angle. The crates were modified by fitting a sloped sheet of metal into the bottom, so that as the crate emptied, the components slid slowly forward to the front where they could be picked out easily by the operator without reaching or bending.

 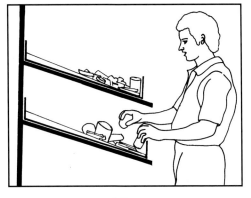

Before   *After*

   This solution has been applied to many crates across the factory. It was achieved at no extra cost to the company, as the metal used to modify the crates was scrap produced by other parts of the factory and cut to the appropriate size.

RESULTS   Upper limb discomfort associated with this task has been reduced.

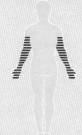

Upper limb

Awkward posture

*Workspace organisation
Component design*

MANY INDUSTRIES HAVE CRATES LOADED WITH MATERIALS FOR USE ON PRODUCTION AND ASSEMBLY LINES. OFTEN REACHING FOR THE LAST FEW COMPONENTS IN A CRATE MEANS THE OPERATOR HAS TO STRETCH AWKWARDLY. THIS SIMPLE SOLUTION CAN BE USED IN MANY SITUATIONS INVOLVING SMALL, LIGHT COMPONENTS.

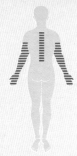

*Upper limb
Back*

Awkward posture

*Workspace organisation
Tool design*

WELDING WORKSTATIONS ARE COMMON THROUGHOUT THE CAR INDUSTRY AND OTHER HEAVY INDUSTRIES. REDESIGNING THE WORKSTATION CAN BENEFIT OPERATORS' POSTURE AND PRODUCT QUALITY.

TASK   Operators at a car manufacturing plant spot welded car body parts at a workstation with a tilted jig to hold the part. The task sequence was:
- the operator loads a body panel into the jig and clamps it into place;
- the operator pulls down a suspended weld gun and spot welds parts into place;
- the gun retracts;
- the operator removes the part.
  The operator did this task about fifty times an hour.

PROBLEM   All staff working in the area were unhappy with the layout, and several experienced discomfort to the arms and back.

ASSESSING THE RISKS AND FINDING SOLUTIONS   The jig was at a 30° angle with a solid frame, so the operator had to lean into the jig and drop the panel onto its location points. This poor posture presented a risk of back injury. Handling the large 10 kg panel presented a risk of musculoskeletal damage. During the welding, the operator had to stretch to the extremities of the jig to weld. This caused strain on the back, arms and hamstrings from pulling on the suspended weld gun. Because of the angle of the jig, the operator had to apply more pressure at the lower points.

The jig was redesigned to improve the operators' access and posture. Changes included:
- raising and horizontally mounting the jig to reduce the forward bending while welding;
- removing a bar at the front of the frame, allowing the operator to stand centrally;
- repositioning the clamps which held the part in place from the inside to the outside of the jig;
- tilting the handles to the welding gun, making them more comfortable to hold;
- improving the flexibility of the welding gun at its suspension joint.

Before

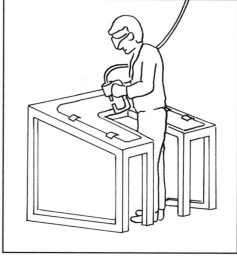

After

The changes were made by an in-house Kaizen (continuous improvement) team. The material costs were approximately £200 and six working days were required for the development and manufacture in-house. The benefits of the redesign include that:

. there is no need to stretch to place and weld parts, so risks of back and arm injury are reduced;

. there is no need to pull on the suspended weld gun because the weight of the gun is balanced for the horizontal jig;

. operators are better protected from sparks from the welding gun.

RESULTS Operators at the workstation now find the welding task much easier and jigs in similar workstations have also been modified in this way. There have been no musculoskeletal complaints since the change. Quality has improved because the operator has a better view of the work piece; this means more accurate spot welds and less damage to the parts.

GENERAL DUTIES USING A VDU

Neck

Awkward posture

Workspace organisation
Workstation design

IT IS ESSENTIAL THAT THE HEIGHT OF A **VDU** SCREEN IS RIGHT FOR THE USER. SCREEN HEIGHT AND ANGLE SHOULD ALLOW A COMFORTABLE HEAD POSITION. NORMALLY THIS MEANS THAT EYES SHOULD BE ABOUT LEVEL WITH THE TOP OF THE SCREEN. EXCEPTIONALLY TALL OR SHORT USERS MAY HAVE OTHER PROBLEMS WITH **VDU** WORKSTATIONS, EG THEY MAY LACK LEGROOM, OR NEED A FOOT REST. IT IS IMPORTANT TO CONSIDER THE USER'S PARTICULAR NEEDS WHEN ASSESSING **VDU** WORKSTATIONS.

TASK   A tall male engineer's job involved daily use of a VDU.

PROBLEM   The engineer had developed pains in his neck. His doctor had advised him to wear a neck collar.

ASSESSING THE RISKS AND FINDING SOLUTIONS   The workstation was assessed to see if the problem could be removed by redesigning the layout of the equipment. The workstation was not properly adjusted to accommodate the engineer's exceptional height. The VDU screen was much lower than his head, causing him to bend his neck down to view the screen.

The screen was raised to improve the angle of his head. This was done simply and cheaply by placing the screen on a shelf.

Before

After

RESULTS   Within a few days the engineer was able to remove his neck collar and work normally. Had the problem persisted, long-term health problems might have resulted, leading to loss of efficiency, sickness absence, staff retraining costs and a potential compensation claim.

SECRETARIAL DUTIES USING A VDU

TASK An employee's general secretarial duties included typing, filing and clerical work. She had a typewriter, but used a VDU workstation (computer screen, keyboard and mouse) for most of her work.

PROBLEM The employee had had discomfort in her neck and right wrist for some time. She had had three months off work.

ASSESSING THE RISKS AND FINDING SOLUTIONS When the employee returned to work her manager asked in-house ergonomists to redesign the layout of her workstation to make her as comfortable as possible and prevent the problem recurring. Problems were identified:

- the chair was too high for the desk, so the employee was working with her arms out too straight and her wrists bent too far upwards to reach the keyboard. Her neck was bent downwards to see the VDU screen;
- the seat was too deep for the employee, so she couldn't comfortably use the backrest for support;
- the split-level surface of the desk top restricted how the equipment and documents could be arranged. So, for example documents had to be placed flat on the desk, with the employee lifting her head up and down to type from them and look at the screen. The lack of surface space also meant that there was not enough room in front of the keyboard to rest her wrists between typing.

Before

It was agreed that the workstation should be rearranged and some new equipment introduced - a height-adjustable chair; a wrist rest; a trackerball; a larger flat desk and a document holder.

RESULTS With a lower chair height, the employee could work comfortably with her elbow angle at about 90°, her wrists about straight and her eyes about level with the top of the screen. She could also sit comfortably using the backrest.

With a new desk, the VDU equipment was better arranged and the document holder reduced the neck turning and bending. The wrist rest allowed the employee to rest her wrists during pauses at the keyboard. The trackerball had a built-in padded area to support the hand and reduce fatigue. It took up less desk space than a

After

Neck
Wrist

Awkward posture

Workspace organisation
Workstation design
Tool design

THE SEAT AND WORKSTATION HEIGHT AT ANY COMPUTER WORKSTATION SHOULD BE COMPATIBLE SO THAT USERS CAN WORK IN SAFE AND COMFORTABLE POSTURES. DOCUMENT HOLDERS ARE A GOOD WAY OF REMOVING AWKWARD AND REPETITIVE HEAD MOVEMENTS WHEN THE USER NEEDS TO LOOK AT DOCUMENTS AND THE SCREEN.

mouse and unlike a mouse did not need use of the whole arm to move it. The thumb could be used for the most common functions, reducing the stress to the fingers. It was also possible to assign functions to any of the trackerball keys so the employee could choose the most comfortable key to use. She found it much less of a strain to use than the mouse.

The layout was altered. The desks were rearranged so that she only had to turn 90° instead of 180° to move from her work desk to the VDU, and the VDU desk was placed at 90° to the window to reduce glare from the sun on the VDU screen.

The employee has had no prolonged period away from work due to wrist or neck problems since the changes. The trackerball was so successful it has been recommended to and used by other ULD sufferers. The new equipment cost about £400. Benefits included an end to the costs of hiring temporary staff, and the associated loss of efficiency and quality. Medical and legal costs which might have been incurred if the problem had developed further were avoided.

VDU OPERATION

TASK A news agency employee used a VDU for about 70% of the day to download, input and verify numerical information. He was right-handed and used a mouse much of the time.

PROBLEM The individual got pain in the top of his right arm and shoulder.

ASSESSING THE RISKS AND FINDING SOLUTIONS Because of the way the equipment was laid out at the workstation, the employee's posture was uncomfortable and restricted. The monitor was in the right-hand corner of the workstation, but the mouse and mouse pad were left of the keyboard. Being right-handed, the employee reached across his body every time he used the mouse. It was difficult to sit like this for long periods, and frequently reaching across his body posed a risk of injury.

Before

Looking at the whole workstation, it was also clear that when the employee was sitting at a comfortable typing height with his arms about flat and level with the work surface, his feet didn't reach the floor. This put pressure on the back of his legs and made sitting uncomfortable.

The equipment was rearranged. The VDU monitor was put on the left side of the workstation, and the mouse on the right of the keyboard, so the employee no longer had to reach across his body. A foot rest was found to support his legs.

After

RESULTS The employee felt more comfortable overall, and the painful symptoms in his right shoulder have gone.

Shoulder
Arm

Awkward posture

Workspace organisation

THE ARRANGEMENT OF EQUIPMENT IN A WORKSTATION IS ONE OF THE KEY THINGS THAT DECIDES THE WORKER'S POSTURE. IT IS ALSO A PART OF THE WORK ENVIRONMENT - ESPECIALLY IN OFFICES - THAT THE WORKER CAN CHANGE TO GET MORE COMFORTABLE. IT COSTS NOTHING. THIS EXAMPLE SHOWS HOW SIMPLE REARRANGEMENTS BY THE WORKER CAN HAVE A BIG IMPACT ON COMFORT. THIS OFTEN LEADS TO HIGHER PRODUCTIVITY AND QUALITY.

WIRE HARNESS OPERATION

Upper limb

Awkward posture

Workspace organisation
Workstation design

TASK Operators at a helicopter manufacturing plant assembled a wire harness at a workstation consisting of a near upright board into which they attached and strung wires. Around 300 workers had to loop different gauge wires through loops built into the boards. Once the wires were routed, they were fitted with plugs, pins and connection devices. Operators worked on the boards in eight hour shifts.

PROBLEM There were many cases of upper limb disorders.

ASSESSING THE RISKS AND FINDING SOLUTIONS

Hazard/risk	*Solution*
Operators had to reach, bend and stretch to access all areas of the wire harness, and their tools. They often had to hold awkward positions for a long time while wiring. This caused fatigue and a risk of upper limb problems.	The workstation was reorganised so that the main tools are nearer and in easy reach. A set of height adjustable suspension frames were also introduced. They cost £1600 each. Operators can now easily raise or lower the board to position their work area at the right height in front of them. This also removes awkward bending and reaching.

RESULTS A trial was performed with the employees using the new workstation for about 30 days. Employees said that they felt much better after the test period and were reluctant to go back to the old system. Long-term savings, in terms of reduced injuries and absenteeism, are expected.

Before

LOADING PRODUCE TRAYS INTO A DELIVERY VAN

TASK   Trays of produce were placed on three tiers of racks in the back of a large van.

PROBLEM   The loading step at the back of the van was long enough for staff to reach only the middle tier of racking without stretching.

Before

After

ASSESSING THE RISKS AND FINDING SOLUTIONS   To reach the racks at either side, staff had to stretch sideways without falling from the step. Handling the trays this way put an uneven strain on the body which could result in back injury, or other injuries from falling off the step.

   The step was extended to the full width of the van. Costs were minimal as the alteration was carried out in-house.

RESULTS   Staff no longer have to stretch awkwardly and risk an accident or injury. The task was carried out more efficiently.

Back

*Awkward posture
Manual handling*

Workstation design

IT IS IMPORTANT IN ANY HANDLING TASK TO HAVE STABLE FOOTING THAT IS LARGE ENOUGH. A LOADING STEP CAN BE HELPFUL FOR THE MANUAL LOADING AND UNLOADING OF ROAD HAULAGE VEHICLES.

Back

*Manual handling
Awkward posture*

Workstation design

HANDLING ELDERLY OR INFIRM PATIENTS IS COMMON IN HOSPITALS AND CARE HOMES. IMPROVING EXISTING AIDS CAN HELP REDUCE RISKS TO CARE ASSISTANTS.

TASK Geriatric or infirm patients with limited mobility can have difficulty getting themselves to the toilet. Hospital staff regularly had to assist patients manually.

PROBLEM Handling patients in the confined toilet space presented risk of back injury.

| *Before* | *After* |

ASSESSING THE RISKS AND FINDING SOLUTIONS The ward sister realised that there was a problem. The limited space made it difficult for the staff to adopt a good posture to assist patients, and the sustained effort needed for many heavy patients made this worse. The sister consulted her staff on what could be done. The toilets already had handles situated on either side to help the patients position themselves, but they were not within easy reach.

Many of the patients were only partially infirm and improving the handles would allow some of them to support themselves much more. A longer retractable handle was introduced to one side of the toilet so that patients could lift themselves up using both hands. A vertical handle was introduced so that patients could hold onto it and pull themselves to their feet using their arms.

RESULTS This allowed many patients to raise themselves with little or no assistance, and allowed more of them to toilet by themselves. Staff found it much easier to handle many patients and were pleased with the results. The risk of injury was considerably reduced. The changes led to an increase in the number of patients who could toilet themselves, adding to their feeling of independence.

HANDLING INFIRM PATIENTS IN A BATHROOM AREA

TASK   Nursing staff had to assist infirm patients when they had a bath. Staff had to support them to the bathroom area and assist them in and out of the bath.

PROBLEM   Patients could be awkward to handle and heavy, presenting a considerable risk of back injury. There was not enough room to use the ward's patient hoist. The bath was against the wall and nurses could not get on either side to assist patients.

ASSESSING THE RISKS AND FINDING SOLUTIONS   The nursing staff felt there was not enough space to handle the patients. It was difficult for more than one nurse to handle patients, and for them to get into the right position for lifting. The ward sister, in consultation with staff, the health and safety adviser and the moving and handling co-ordinator, proposed changes to the bathroom area layout to make handling the patients easier.

More space was created by replacing the partitions with curtains. The patients kept their privacy, but the staff had easier access to manoeuvre them. The bath was moved further away from the wall, giving room to use the patient hoist, and staff could get to both sides of the bath.

Back

Manual handling
Awkward posture

Workstation design
Mechanisation

IT IS IMPORTANT THAT ENOUGH SPACE IS PROVIDED FOR HANDLING AIDS TO BE USED WHEREVER POSSIBLE, AND THAT STAFF ARE IN THE RIGHT POSITION AND POSTURE WHEN LIFTING.

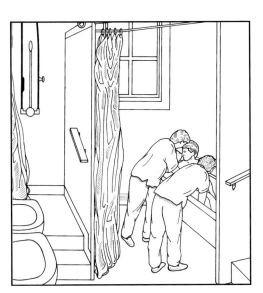

Before

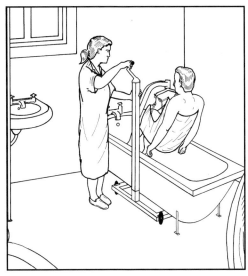

After

RESULTS   The changes cost between £2500 and £3000 per ward and included replacing the flooring, redecorating the area and modifying the toilets to improve access. The risk of back injury was substantially reduced. Increasing the amount of space also allowed two nurses to assist the patient instead of one, allowed the hoist to be used, and meant patients could manoeuvre themselves more easily.

BAGGAGE HANDLING

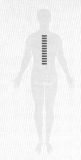

Back

Manual handling
Awkward posture

Workstation design

MODIFICATIONS LIKE THIS MAY BE USEFUL IN ANY INDUSTRIAL OPERATION WHERE ITEMS OF DIFFERENT SIZES, SHAPES AND WEIGHT ARE HANDLED ON OR OFF CONVEYORS AND INTO OR OUT OF TROLLEYS OR CONTAINERS. IT IS IMPORTANT TO MAXIMISE THE BENEFIT BY ADOPTING ERGONOMIC PRINCIPLES WITHIN COMPANY STANDARDS OR POLICIES FOR FUTURE USE.

TASK Baggage handlers at an airport moved baggage to or from baggage conveyors and containers.

PROBLEM The handlers suffered significant periods of sickness absence due to back pain. In 1988 about 20% of the workforce took sickness absence for this reason, and the average length of absence was 22 days.

ASSESSING THE RISKS AND FINDING SOLUTIONS

Hazard/risk	*Solution*
Weight of the baggage unknown, making it difficult to prepare properly for the lift.	A policy of labelling baggage weighing more than 25 kg was introduced.
The height and position of the conveyors varied, and the job involved repetitive twisting, reaching and stooping.	The height of the conveyors was standardised to 650 mm to reduce the amount of stooping. Simple modifications were made on the high throughput conveyors to control the orientation of the baggage better. Tilted conveyors were changed to flat ones, so that baggage could be more easily moved.
Distribution of tasks and workloads between teams of handlers was uneven, leaving some teams more at risk of injury.	More efficient control and use of staff was introduced. Greater attention was paid to the need to spread the workload during manual handling training.

Before

After

These solutions were built into the design of new installations as part of a major extension of the airport, so costs were negligible. Modification of 19 existing conveyors to meet the new specification cost 7% of the annual engineering budget for the airport.

RESULTS

- Manual handling sickness absence reduced by 77% over the last four years.
- A major union complaint resolved and industrial relations improved.
- A fitter workforce.
- An Engineering Standard produced for the design of future installations.

RACKING OPERATIONS IN DRYING ROOM

Knee

Awkward posture

Workstation design

IMPROVING EMPLOYEE POSTURE AND COMFORT CAN OFTEN BE DONE BY CHANGING THE HEIGHTS AT WHICH MATERIALS ARE STORED. THIS PRINCIPLE CAN BE APPLIED, OFTEN FOR LITTLE COST, TO MANY WORK OPERATIONS.

TASK   At a surgical supplies manufacturing plant, employees hung bundles of surgical thread strands from a rack to dry. The strands were suspended on poles which slotted into holes in a racking system from 30 cm above the floor and 2 m high. As part of the process, the operators pulled on the strands and put combs along the length of the pole to separate the individual strands to speed drying. It took about six minutes to suspend each set of poles and separate the strands.

PROBLEM   Some operators complained of sore knees and fatigue.

ASSESSING THE RISKS AND FINDING SOLUTIONS   Racking the strands nearest the floor presented a risk of injury because the operator had to stoop to pull the strands and insert the combs. Maintaining this poor posture for long periods presented a risk of injury, particularly to the back and knees. To reduce the stooping, the lower levels of the racking were removed. The height was set so that the racking was done at or above the operator's knuckle height, cutting out the stooping. Because there was enough storage space, this solution was implemented at no extra cost.

Before

RESULTS   Removing the stooping reduced the risk of injury. The racking was also done more quickly, as it had taken longer to work on the lower levels. Operators reported that the job was easier, less stressful on the knees, and less tiring.

After

COMPUTER DISK DRIVE ASSEMBLY

TASK   Operators in a computer manufacturing firm worked on a conveyor assembly line making disk drives. The line was imported from a sister factory in Japan, and the production method had been modified to involve less automation and more operators. Tasks included driving screws with suspended powered screwdrivers.

PROBLEM   Company records showed that about half of the reports to the medical department from operators on this line related to neck pain, and half to wrist pain. On a similar line of a slightly different size and layout, neck pain accounted for only a quarter of medical reports.

Neck
Wrist

ASSESSING THE RISKS AND FINDING SOLUTIONS   Because the conveyor had been designed for Japanese operators, and the Japanese population is generally smaller than the European population, the height of the

Awkward posture

conveyor was too low for most of the operators in the UK site. They had to stoop and work in an uncomfortable position, also tilting their heads forward. This was made worse by service units under the conveyor, the conveyor depth, and assembly pallets which ran on it. Several operators who couldn't fit their legs under the conveyor, were sitting further away from the work and had to bend even

Before   *After*

Workstation design

further forward. It was not possible to raise the height of the conveyor as other automated parts of the line were of fixed heights.

A new conveyor was purpose-built to assemble the next version of the product, but designed to avoid the problems associated with the imported line. A conveyor height of 1000 mm allowed operators to choose whether to work sitting or standing. The conveyor and the assembly pallets were narrower so the operator had more leg-room. The trays for the parts were angled directly in front of the operator, and further adjustments to the size of the conveyor frame could be made if necessary. Because the improved features were incorporated at the design specification stage, there was no additional cost.

IT IS IMPORTANT TO CONSIDER THE SIZE OF THE POPULATION WHICH WILL BE USING A WORKSTATION, PARTICULARLY WHERE WORKSTATIONS ARE IMPORTED. INCORPORATING ERGONOMICS INTO PLANNED CHANGES AND NEW DESIGNS WHENEVER POSSIBLE REMOVES THE NEED FOR AND COST OF LATER IMPROVEMENTS.

RESULTS   Operators at the new line perform similar assembly tasks, but are more upright and comfortable. The improvements are expected to lead to a reduction in injuries in time.

MATERIAL STORAGE

Back
Shoulder

Awkward posture

Workstation design

REMEMBER TO CONSIDER THE SIZE OF EMPLOYEES AND HOW FAR THEY CAN COMFORTABLY REACH FOR COMPONENTS, TOOLS ETC. **S**TRETCHING AND AWKWARD POSTURES CONTRIBUTE TO UPPER LIMB DISORDERS AND BACK PROBLEMS.

TASK At a car interiors assembly plant, clips and other components were assembled onto instrument panels. Operators had to reach for components from storage bins around their workstations.

PROBLEM There were reports of fatigue and discomfort in operators' backs and shoulders.

ASSESSING THE RISKS AND FINDING SOLUTIONS Many of the bins were located unnecessarily high and far away from the operators, often causing extreme stretching and awkward back and shoulder postures.

Lowered and angled shelves were provided across the plant. In some areas, carousel designs and gravity shelves have been installed to make components easier to reach. Changes to the component storage cost £60.

RESULTS Shoulder and back postures have improved throughout the plant, and the experience gained will be helpful in future workstation designs. The operators have reported less fatigue and discomfort.

Before

After

COMPUTER HARD DISK WORKSTATION

Before   After

Back
Shoulder

Awkward posture

Workstation design

TASK At a large computer manufacturing firm, newly assembled hard disks were formatted at a workstation imported from a sister factory in Japan. Throughout the day operators would insert the disks into the machine.

PROBLEM Operators in this area reported back and shoulder soreness.

ASSESSING THE RISKS AND FINDING SOLUTIONS The height of the workstation was too low for most operators. This caused them to stoop slightly each time they inserted or removed a disk.

For a minimal cost, the workstation was raised 10 cm (with leg extensions), so the operators could reach the equipment more comfortably and without stooping.

RESULTS Operators are more comfortable and reports of back and shoulder soreness have reduced. The company prevented the problems getting worse, and avoided costs from staff absence and sick pay.

IT IS IMPORTANT TO DESIGN WORK SURFACES AT THE RIGHT HEIGHT SO THEY ARE COMFORTABLE FOR OPERATORS. THIS PRINCIPLE APPLIES TO MANY INDUSTRIAL WORKSTATIONS.

WASHING UTENSILS IN A SINK

Shoulder
Neck
Back

Awkward posture

Workstation design

TASK Staff in a hospital had to wash a variety of basins and containers for several hours a day.

PROBLEM Because of the shape and size of the basins the shallow sink that had previously been used was inadequate. A new, deep, double sink was installed, but soon afterwards staff complained of pains in the shoulders, neck and back.

ASSESSING THE RISKS AND FINDING SOLUTIONS The local manager spoke to the health and safety adviser who agreed with the staff's view that the new sink had not been installed at the right height for the task. Because the sink was too low, staff were constantly reaching below their waist height and working with their arms too far away from their bodies. This was putting strain on different parts of their upper bodies.

   The health and safety adviser conducted a number of trials so that staff could say what height sink was most comfortable for them. As a result, the sink was raised by about 25 cm.

RESULTS
*   Reduction in the number of staff complaints.
*   Increased staff morale.
*   Reduced risk of injury.

Before

After

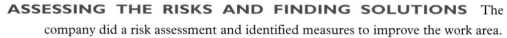

CONTROL BOX ASSEMBLY

TASK   Operators at a refrigeration manufacturing plant performed wiring operations on electrical control boxes at a standing workstation. They used powered hand-tools in the assembly of the boxes which were about 72 cm^2.

PROBLEM   Several operators complained of fatigue and discomfort in the lower back, and some attempted to improve their work area by standing on home-made platforms.

ASSESSING THE RISKS AND FINDING SOLUTIONS   The company did a risk assessment and identified measures to improve the work area.

    The workstation was at a fixed height and to do some of the assembly using the power tools, the operators had to hold their bodies and wrists in awkward and uncomfortable positions. They also had to lean forward to reach all areas of the unit.

    To get rid of these awkward postures - the likely cause of the back pain - a new assembly fixture was developed and incorporated into a change to the production process. The control box was mounted on this fixture which could be raised, lowered and rotated away from the operators, giving them easier access to each side of the unit. The fixtures cost about £950 each to implement as part of an overall production line change.

RESULTS   By changing the position of the piece being assembled, the operator could reach it more easily and work in a more upright posture with straighter wrists. Complaints of fatigue and discomfort have fallen and the assembly is now performed slightly faster.

    The control box which weighs over 20 kg is now lifted once rather than six times, as the adjustable fixture was designed to be easily pushed from operation to operation.

Lower back

Awkward posture

Workstation design

ADJUSTABILITY IN A WORKSTATION CAN GREATLY IMPROVE AN OPERATOR'S POSTURE. IN ORDER TO ENSURE THAT THE OPERATORS ACTUALLY MAKE THE PROPER ADJUSTMENTS, IT IS IMPORTANT THAT THE ADJUSTMENT MECHANISMS ARE EASY TO USE.

Before

After

PACKING ON A PRODUCTION LINE

Upper limbs

Awkward posture

Workstation design
Task design

IT IS IMPORTANT TO MIX
ERGONOMIC PRINCIPLES WITH
GOOD MANUFACTURING AND
PERSONNEL PRACTICES.

Before

TASK Staff on a factory production line were packing biscuits.

PROBLEM The management team identified a series of initial problems affecting the health of staff and the productivity of a particular department. They found symptoms of upper limb disorder, nausea, dizziness, a high accident rate and high staff turnover. Despite these problems, they had to increase productivity within a year.

ASSESSING THE RISKS AND FINDING SOLUTIONS The management team recognised that the situation was serious and that accidents and ill health were inevitable unless they made significant improvements. Without these, they could not achieve increased productivity. A project team was established to make key decisions. They recognised a need for a major investment in redesign, called in ergonomists to identify specific problems and advise on redesign, consulted staff, increased the ratio of trainers to operatives, and gave a performance briefing to staff.

Solutions were recommended to deal with particular problems.

Hazard/risk	*Solution*
Upper conveyor too high, causing stretching above shoulder height.	Reduce conveyor height.
Containers too far away, causing reaching and stretching.	Reduce width of conveyor and allow containers to overlap it.
Lower conveyor too low, leading to stooped back posture.	Raise conveyor.

After

Standing for long periods, causing discomfort and fatigue.	Provide appropriate seating, foot bar or anti-fatigue matting.
Waste put in box under lower conveyor, leading to awkward bending and stooping.	Provide waste chute within easy reach.

A mock-up of an adjustable workstation was made to try different designs. Staff gave their preferences for different layouts and workstation dimensions.

New equipment was installed, work organisation was changed, and training was improved.

RESULTS

- Productivity increased (output up 33% with 25% more operatives).
- Health and safety benefits from reduced line speed (38% speed reduction).
- Product quality improved.
- Labour turnover reduced.
- Accidents significantly reduced.
- Sickness absence reduced.
- Fewer health problems reported (upper limb disorders down 48%, dizziness down 26%).
- General absence reduced.

The payback period of the total investment required was well under three years because of reduced overheads and better productivity. In addition, potential losses arising from accidents, injury and ill health, claims for compensation and consequent increases in insurance costs, were brought under tighter control.

TELEPHONE EXCHANGE EQUIPMENT ASSEMBLY

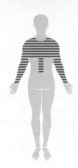

Back
Arm
Shoulder

Awkward posture

Workstation design
Tool design

IT IS IMPORTANT TO MONITOR THE EFFECTS OF ERGONOMIC CHANGES. SICK LEAVE FIGURES ARE A GOOD POINTER TO PROBLEMS. MEASURING SICK LEAVE BEFORE AND AFTER CHANGES ARE MADE CAN HELP SHOW WHETHER THE PROBLEM HAS BEEN SOLVED.

TASK   Full-time operatives, working 8 hour days, assembled telephone exchange equipment. Their main task was joining wires to terminals in an upright frame, 1000 mm wide by 400-800 mm high, using an electric wrapping gun (this spins the wire around the terminal). The frame was supported on a fixed height table.

PROBLEM   A high rate of sick leave, labour turnover and rehabilitation problems had been recorded over a seven year period.

ASSESSING THE RISKS AND FINDING SOLUTIONS   The major cause appeared to be shoulder disorders arising from stress on the shoulder and arm muscles from working in cramped positions. Work on the upper rows of the frame was done standing with the arms and shoulders raised; on the middle rows sitting on a height-adjustable chair; and on the lower rows sitting bent forwards with arms resting on the table.

Management and unions agreed to set up a programme to deal with the problems, including a long-term study of the musculoskeletal illness. Major changes were made to improve the workstation design, giving the operatives a greater choice of work postures:

- the frame was mounted on a hydraulic stand with 600 mm vertical travel, allowing them to work sitting and standing;
- all seated work could be done at about the same height, so the chair could be adjusted to the individual's requirements rather than to task demands;
- the chair had arm rests with adjustable height and slope to reduce stress on the arms, and an effective back rest to give back support;
- a lighter pneumatic wrapping gun was used so that even though standing work was still needed sometimes, the load on the shoulders was much less;
- the frame could also be set lower for standing work, so the operatives needed to stretch less.

The long-term study continued for over nine years with 420 subjects. It included medical examinations, a laboratory study of shoulder muscle activity, measurement of joint angles, and comparison of rates of sick leave and labour turnover, before and after the workstation redesign.

RESULTS

- Sick leave due to musculoskeletal problems was reduced by more than 92%.
- The steady increase in musculoskeletal-related sick leave stopped sharply after the changes, and productivity increased.
- Labour turnover reduced by nearly 75%.

The savings arising from the changes (reduced recruitment costs, training, and sick leave), outweighed the company's investment nearly ten times.

SPRING BRAKE ACTUATOR ASSEMBLY

TASK   Spring brake actuators are designed to perform the functions of normal service braking together with the emergency and parking brake on large vehicles. Several components make up the actuators which are assembled largely by hand. One of the assembly tasks involved pushing down hard on a sprung push-plate until the spring was compressed below the 'split line' where the operator used a foot treadle to operate a collar gripping mechanism to hold the assembly in place. Then the diaphragm, air pressure plate and clamp ring were put in place and tightened. Between 60 and 70 of these were assembled per day.

PROBLEM   The considerable force needed to push down on the spring and push-plate led to shoulder and upper arm discomfort among the operators. There was also a risk of a serious accident. If the collar gripping mechanism failed, the operator would be hit in the face by the components, ejected by the force of the spring releasing.

ASSESSING THE RISKS AND FINDING SOLUTIONS   The actuator department team wanted to remove the possibility of an accident. The workstations were altered so that the push-plate was fitted into a 'head assembly rig', with an air ram above. Thus the operation of manually pushing down on the push-plate is removed, as is the risk of an accident. The total cost of equipping each rig was £6600, with a one-off design cost of £2800. Seven assembly rigs were modified.

RESULTS

- The risk of accident from this operation has been removed.
- The manual force and risk of injury and discomfort to the shoulder and upper arms has been removed.
- Less fatigue has meant that more actuators can be assembled per day when orders require.
- The task is 'easier', and operators no longer see it as unpleasantly dangerous.

Shoulder Arm

Applied force

Workstation design

THE MAIN REASON FOR EQUIPPING THESE WORKSTATIONS WITH THE HEAD ASSEMBLY RIG AND AIR RAM WAS TO REMOVE THE POSSIBILITY OF ACCIDENT. BUT THE MODIFICATIONS ALSO REMOVED THE RISK OF UPPER LIMB DISCOMFORT AND INJURY. ALTHOUGH EXPENSIVE, THE CHANGES TO THE WORKSTATIONS HAVE COMPLETELY ELIMINATED TWO HIGH-RISK ACTIVITIES FROM THE ASSEMBLY OPERATION.

Elbow
Shoulder

Repetition
Applied force
Awkward posture

✓

Workstation design
Machinery design

INSPECTION AND TESTING TASKS IN SEVERAL INDUSTRIES CAN BE VERY REPETITIVE, AND IF POOR POSTURES OR HIGH FORCES ARE ALSO PART OF THE TASK, THE RISK OF MUSCULOSKELETAL INJURY CAN BE HIGH. AS WITH MOST TASKS, EFFECTIVE SOLUTIONS CAN BE FOUND, BASED ON A GOOD ASSESSMENT OF THE TASK WHICH FINDS THE RISK FACTORS.

TASK An operator in the car industry tested product quality at three covered test stands. For each test they lifted the test stand cover, from waist level to overhead, inserted the product and closed the cover. Operators did this about 2000 times in each 10 hour shift.

PROBLEM Some operators had reported pain in the elbow and shoulder regions.

ASSESSING THE RISKS AND FINDING SOLUTIONS Several factors contributed to the risk of long-term shoulder and arm injuries:
- the short cycle time of the test made the task very repetitive;
- the fairly high force (10-12 kg) needed to lift and lower the cover;
- the awkward arm posture when the cover was open;
- the high speed movement and slowing of the arm associated with opening and closing the cover.

Before

The test stand was redesigned and semi-automated so the operator no longer had to open and close the cover. All three stands were enclosed in a booth. The operator sat inside the semi-automatic test stand, removed the parts after the test and put them in a container, depending on whether they passed or failed the test. The change cost about £20 000.

RESULTS
- The repetitive high speed, forceful arm movements were eliminated and operators reported a drop in the painful symptoms in the elbows and shoulders.
- Productivity increased by approximately 6%.

AEROSPACE ASSEMBLY TASK

TASK An operator at an aerostructure manufacturing plant worked for an entire eight hour shift at a dimpler machine (a press which produces a small dent in the panels for the outer surface of the aeroplane so that the rivets will be flush with the surface). The dimpler machine was activated using a foot control. The operator used a box about six inches high as a footrest when seated. There was also a table to one side of the machine.

PROBLEM The last operator doing this task had suffered an injury diagnosed as cumulative rotator cuff syndrome for which she had needed surgery. A review of the injury and illness records showed that this task resulted in 167 lost work days and a total cost to the company of over £50 000. A new operator was assigned to the workstation. In the 13 months since taking the position she had reported to the medical department nine times with pains in the wrist and shoulder, and wore a wrist brace.

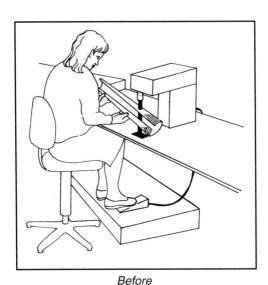

Before

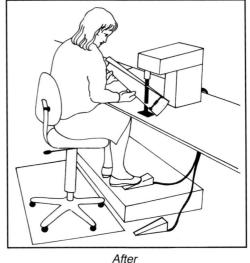

After

PUNCH PRESS OPERATIONS ARE COMMON IN SEVERAL MANUFACTURING INDUSTRIES. IMPROVEMENTS IN THE OPERATOR'S POSTURE CAN OFTEN BE MADE BY IMPROVED SEATING AND WORKSTATION LAYOUT; PHYSICAL STRESS CAN BE REDUCED BY PROVIDING SUITABLE TOOLS.

ASSESSING THE RISKS AND FINDING SOLUTIONS An assessment of the task and workstation revealed several risk factors, including:
- one of the parts used was a curved leading edge to an aeroplane wingflap. Operators had to pull the curved edge open and at the same time use a strong gripping and pulling force to line up the part beneath the machine. This combined with poor wrist postures presented a risk of wrist injury. The difficulty of this operation increased the time the task needed and affected the quality of the work;
- many of the parts were very long. The operators had to balance a part with one hand while aligning it with the dimpler machine. This was time-consuming, difficult and fatiguing;
- the table next to the machine was too high and put the part at a tilt if the operator rested it on the table;

- the operator's chair had no castors and the backrest was not height-adjustable. The operator sat on the front edge of the chair with a cushion beneath her. She could not move the chair forwards because the footrest box was in the way;

- the operator had one foot control which she had to move from the footrest to the floor when changing from sitting to standing.

Several changes were made to the workstation to reduce the risks, including providing:

- **a** more supportive adjustable chair;

- a tool to spread and hold open the curved leading edge part, so the operator did not need to pull it open;

- a second foot control: one for when seated and another for standing;

- a lower table next to the machine. The operator could rest the heavy long parts on the table to support the weight while using the machine.

- an anti-fatigue mat in front of the machine to relieve the stress on the lower limbs when standing.

The changes cost about £650.

RESULTS   The operator's posture has improved with a better chair and lower table. Most importantly, the need to pull the curved elevator part open was removed by using the spreading tool. Feedback from the operator has been very positive, and reports of discomfort to the medical department have dropped. The changes are expected to improve production time and quality aspects of the job.

GEAR AND COVER ASSEMBLY

TASK At a car parts assembly plant a seated operator used a sealing press during gear assembly. She performed the following cycle approximately 117 times an hour while the assembly pallet was in the press:

- place gear in housing assembly;
- put lubricating grease over gear;
- insert washer over centre of gear assembly;
- place gasket to line outside of housing assembly;
- place cover assembly over gasket;
- activate press to seal entire assembly.

Before

PROBLEM Several operators on this task complained how awkward the task was and the workstation was often a bottle-neck on the assembly line.

ASSESSING THE RISKS AND FINDING SOLUTIONS The press itself obstructed the operators' view and forced them into a very awkward back and neck posture. In addition, they worked with bent wrists and had to use pinch grips on the parts. There was a clear risk of upper limb disorders and back problems developing.

After

The workstation was modified so that the operator assembled the parts at a station immediately before the sealing press on the assembly line. This eliminated the need to bend to the side to see the assembly and allowed parts and materials to be stored in front of the operator. A presence sensing switch was installed at the press so that when the assembly pallet passed over it, the cycle for the press began automatically. The modification cost approximately £300 for the cabling, switches and labour time. The changes were made outside working hours and there was no lost production.

RESULTS

- The changes to the workstation improved the operator's posture and reduced the number of awkward wrist positions combined with pinch grips (by 69% for the right hand).
- Storing the materials in front of the operator eliminated the twisting to retrieve materials and bending to activate the control.
- Line production increased by 33%, removing the assembly line bottleneck.
- Feedback from the operators indicated that the changes have greatly improved their overall comfort, and reduced the risk of injury. Complaints due to poor posture have stopped.

Upper limb
Back

Awkward posture
Grip

Workstation design
Machinery design
Task design

PRESS OPERATIONS ARE COMMON IN SEVERAL MANUFACTURING INDUSTRIES. REARRANGING THE WORKSTATION AFTER A RISK ASSESSMENT CAN IMPROVE OPERATOR COMFORT AND REDUCE THE RISK OF UPPER LIMB DISORDERS AND OTHER INJURIES. OPERATORS OFTEN ACHIEVE GREATER PRODUCTIVITY AT A MORE COMFORTABLE WORKSTATION.

ELECTRONICS ASSEMBLY

*Shoulder
Neck*

Awkward posture

Workstation design

IT IS IMPORTANT THAT
WORKSTATIONS CAN BE
ADJUSTED TO SUIT OPERATORS
OF DIFFERENT HEIGHTS, AND
AVOID AWKWARD POSTURES THAT
CAN LEAD TO MUSCULOSKELETAL
PROBLEMS. EXISTING
WORKSTATIONS CAN OFTEN BE
MODIFIED FOR LITTLE COST -
PURCHASING NEW WORKSTATIONS
MAY NOT BE NECESSARY.
ANTI-FATIGUE MATS CAN BE USED
TO REDUCE LEG DISCOMFORT
WHEN EMPLOYEES ARE STANDING
ON HARD SURFACES FOR LONG
PERIODS.

TASK Operators assembled transformers and other components into a metal casting. The fully assembled casting weighed about 60 kg and systems were in place to minimise its handling. The casting was held in a special rotation fixture so it could be turned part way and held securely, giving operators easier access to the opening at the top. The unit was assembled on a fixed height table so the operators could move the fixture and casting to other trolleys at the same height, for transportation, by sliding it along rails similar to those on the trolley. Operators usually stood while assembling parts into the casting.

Before

PROBLEM Within two months of setting up the job, operators doing the assembly complained of shoulder and neck pain. They also had tiredness and some discomfort in their legs which they attributed to standing on the hard floor for long periods of time.

ASSESSING THE RISKS AND FINDING SOLUTIONS The operators visited the company occupational health nurse and safety officer, and the job was investigated for potential improvements.

After

The fixed height of the assembly table was too high for several operators, especially the shorter ones. Although the unit could be rotated in the fixture, the height of the table forced some of them to hold their arms up for a long time, creating a risk of upper limb, shoulder and back problems.

A team of safety and engineering staff identified the need to change the table height. They also considered providing platforms for the employees to stand on. They decided against this because of the tripping hazard platforms could present as operators often had to walk around the area to collect parts. Instead, they shortened the legs of the table and installed a £28 car jack. The operators could alter the height to suit them simply by turning a metal bar. Four tables were changed in-house, costing about £200 each for parts and labour. It was agreed that the operators' leg discomfort was due to the hard floor and anti-fatigue mats were introduced.

RESULTS With the operators able to adjust the table height, and so work without raising their arms, there have been no further reports of discomfort. The company prevented the problem worsening and avoided possible costs of operator absence and sick pay.

TIE BAR ASSEMBLY

TASK At a car assembly plant, operators heated strips of rubber on a hot plate in front of their workstation at about shoulder height. They lowered the warmed strips to bench level and put them on a tie bar. They lowered about 40 strips, of no great weight, each hour. At a later stage the operator added clips to the bars which served as attachment points for other components.

PROBLEM Several operators reported shoulder discomfort. At least one person had been injured when the flat screwdriver being used to add the clips had slipped and punctured their other hand.

ASSESSING THE RISKS AND FINDING SOLUTIONS The height of the shelf with the hot plate caused the operator to reach awkwardly to grasp the strip of rubber. The shelf had been fixed at this level to avoid accidental leaning or resting on the hot surface. It was also noticed that operators bent their wrists awkwardly to add the clips, mainly because of the angle of the equipment.

Four main changes were made to the workstation:

- the hot plate was lowered to make it easier to reach. Shields were put on three sides of the shelf to stop accidental burns;
- workstations were made adjustable to cater for height differences between operators. Employees can easily adjust the workstation at the beginning of each shift and throughout the day, so awkward head, arm, shoulder and back postures were reduced;
- the workstation was angled slightly towards the operator to improve visibility while the clips are added, and improve wrist angles;
- better grips were added to the screwdriver to reduce the risk of slippage. These changes cost about £60.

Shoulder

Awkward posture
Grip

Workstation design
Tool design

SEVERAL CHANGES TO THIS WORKSTATION ALL INVOLVED THE PHYSICAL DESIGN OF THE WORKSTATION TO IMPROVE THE WORKER'S POSTURE. GOOD POSTURE IS IMPORTANT IN WORKBENCH ASSEMBLY TASKS IN A WIDE RANGE OF MANUFACTURING INDUSTRIES, AS WELL AS OFFICE TASKS SUCH AS VDU USE.

Before

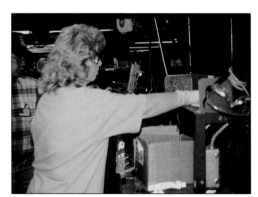

After

RESULTS The number of complaints has reduced and the operators considered the changes a great improvement. The risk of cuts from the screwdriver slipping has been reduced.

Upper limb

Awkward posture

Workstation design

THIS STUDY SHOWS HOW LOW-COST WORKSTATION MODIFICATIONS CAN REDUCE RISKS AND IMPROVE COMFORT. IT ALSO SHOWS THAT IT IS NOT ALWAYS NECESSARY TO BUY EXPENSIVE, NEW EQUIPMENT TO COMPLY WITH REGULATIONS.

Before

After

TASK Secretarial work in an office had changed a lot in ten years, with the move from typewriters to VDUs. About 60% of the secretaries' time is now spent using VDUs. Typewriters are rarely used.

PROBLEM Reports of upper limb discomfort began to increase.

ASSESSING THE RISKS AND FINDING SOLUTIONS The secretaries' desks were ten years old, and although good quality, had been designed for use with typewriters which sat on a 'return' unit 30 mm lower than the main part of the desk. VDUs now sat on the return units, and most staff working with them found it uncomfortable. Because the screen and keyboard were very low, they had to work hunched over. The units were narrow (600 mm), there was little room for the keyboard, and no space to rest wrists.

The purchasing department identified these problems and developed a two-phase modification to solve the problems and comply with the Health and Safety (Display Screen Equipment) Regulations 1992. During an office move, the desks were converted by raising the return units to the same height as the rest of the desk, giving a level L-shaped surface. This meant users could arrange the VDUs more flexibly, and sit more comfortably upright. They could also move the keyboard and rest their arms and hands when they wanted.

For the second modification, an attachment was put on the inside corner of the desk to give a larger surface area. The processor unit and screen could be moved back, and the keyboard was no longer balanced across the inside edges of the desk. It cost £42 to modify each desk - much less than the cost of a new one.

RESULTS Users can now sit properly and are much more comfortable than before. Screens are at comfortable viewing distances in the corner of the workstations and the keyboards can be used in different positions.

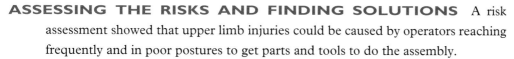

MULTI-FUNCTION PRINTED CIRCUIT BOARD ASSEMBLY

TASK Operators at a helicopter manufacturing plant assembled printed circuit boards. They did various tasks in assembling the boards, but mainly applied pins, plugs and couplers.

PROBLEM There had been many complaints of upper limb pain from the operators.

ASSESSING THE RISKS AND FINDING SOLUTIONS A risk assessment showed that upper limb injuries could be caused by operators reaching frequently and in poor postures to get parts and tools to do the assembly.

A new workstation costing £1250 was provided, with several adjustable components, allowing the operator to do the tasks in a more comfortable position. It included:

- a screwdriver suspended on a moveable arm;
- a rotating and swivelling adaptor bracket to hold the panel being assembled;
- a workstation adjustable in tilt and height;
- a part tray on a moveable arm.

Before

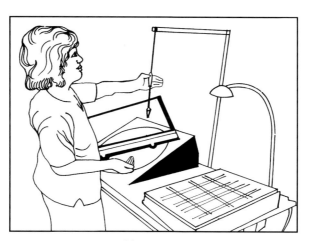

After

RESULTS The new workstations received widespread approval from the employees, and reports of upper limb pain have fallen.

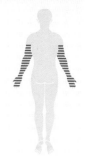

Upper limb

Awkward posture
Repetition

Workstation design
Tool design
Component design

PLACING MICROCHIPS INTO BOARDS IS A VERY COMMON TASK IN THE ELECTRONICS INDUSTRY. BECAUSE OPERATORS ARE OFTEN IN ONE POSITION FOR A LONG TIME, IT IS IMPORTANT THAT THEIR POSTURE IS RIGHT. ADJUSTABILITY IN THE WORKSTATION AND TOOLS WHICH CAN BE EASILY USED BY THE OPERATOR WILL ALLOW THEM TO FIND A COMFORTABLE WORKING POSTURE.

PREPARING WAX PATTERNS FOR ENGINE PARTS MANUFACTURE

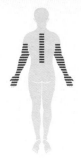

Back
Upper limb

Awkward posture

Workstation design

WHEREVER POSSIBLE, A MOCK-UP OR PROTOTYPE SHOULD BE USED TO EVALUATE PROPOSED WORKSTATION CHANGES. USERS SHOULD BE FULLY INVOLVED IN THE EVALUATION PROCESS. NOT ONLY CAN THE DIMENSIONS BE OPTIMISED, BUT UNNECESSARY FEATURES AND FITTINGS CAN BE ELIMINATED, REDUCING COSTS.

TASK Operatives assembled injection-moulded wax patterns for use in a lost-wax casting process. The pattern components were trimmed and patched and assembled to form the mould, before the wax cores were inserted. The operatives sat at individual workbenches and used heated wax and heated hand tools.

PROBLEM The company was in the process of reviewing workplace design and facilities in this department. They particularly wanted to reduce the risk of musculoskeletal disorders and improve the sickness absence record. Consultant ergonomists were asked to study current work practices and postures and produce an improved workplace design.

ASSESSING THE RISKS AND FINDING SOLUTIONS They assessed the tasks and discussed handling, workplace and environmental aspects with the operatives. Almost half had back or upper limb conditions and all experienced discomfort.

The operatives worked in a variety of awkward postures due to the high work surface, restricted work area and bad seat design.

A prototype workbench with a rolled front edge was designed and constructed. It had features to reduce radiant heat from the heated wax pots, and better task lighting. Under-bench storage drawers, a slide extension, a turntable unit, an adjustable footrest and a fully adjustable seat were provided. Operatives used the prototype bench for up to three days and completed a questionnaire.

Evaluation of the operatives' use of the prototype workstation showed that:
* the reduced worksurface height, although a compromise because the workpiece height varied, was satisfactory at 750 mm;
* with the new workbench height, most operatives needed a footrest. One found that the footrest wasn't high enough;
* one operative found there was not enough leg-room;
* a worksurface area of 1400 mm by 650 mm was enough for the work. A depth of more than 650 mm made it more difficult to reach the back of the bench where the wax pots and hotplate were located;
* a slide-out extension to the worksurface was useful, but some operatives favoured the shaped front of the original bench where they could rest their elbows during fine work;
* the rounded front edge of the prototype workbench made resting arms on the edge much more comfortable;
* the under-bench drawer was useful, but the turntable was disliked;
* the seat was generally liked - particularly the easy adjustment and additional support.

RESULTS These and other results of the prototype evaluation were used to design new workbenches which were successfully installed. Operatives' work postures visibly improved and they were able to work more comfortably. Reports of pain and wrist swelling reduced. The environment was better with improved lighting and less radiant heat.

USE OF AIRPORT CHECK-IN DESKS

TASK Operators at a large international airport checked in airline customers by logging flight and seat information etc onto a computer system.

PROBLEM New VDU equipment had recently been installed by a number of operating companies in the airport. Immediately after the installation five operators complained of neck strain and upper limb discomfort, and there were three lost time injuries.

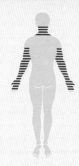

Neck
Upper limb

Repetition
Awkward posture

Before

After

Workstation design
Workspace organisation

ASSESSING THE RISKS AND FINDING SOLUTIONS An assessment of the operators using the check-in desks suggested one main cause of the problems - the display screen monitor sat on a small stem mounted on top of the shelf above the desk, and to one side of the operator. They had to repeatedly twist their necks to look up and view the display.

The operators were provided with height-adjustable chairs. But the range of adjustment was not enough to allow the chairs to be positioned at a height to suit typing and viewing the screen.

To overcome the problem the stem was removed from the display screen, reducing its height by 75 mm. The display could now be positioned nearer the centre of the shelf, reducing the neck twisting and head lifting movements. Possible postural problems for the operator had been considered at the design stage, but the stem which was not part of the original design had been introduced during construction.

RESULTS In the nine months since the changes, there have been no lost time injuries and no complaints of discomfort.

BEFORE BUYING NEW EQUIPMENT, THINK ABOUT POSSIBLE PROBLEMS IN NEW DESIGNS. ADDITIONAL COSTS CAN BE AVOIDED BY CONSIDERING POSSIBLE PROBLEMS FOR THE OPERATOR AT THE DESIGN STAGE. IT IS ALSO IMPORTANT TO ENSURE THAT GOOD ERGONOMIC PRACTICE IS FOLLOWED THROUGHOUT THE DESIGN CYCLE, SO THAT PROBLEMS ARE NOT INADVERTENTLY INTRODUCED.

INTENSIVE KEYBOARD USE

Neck
Lower back
Legs

Awkward posture

Workstation design

SMALL ADJUSTMENTS TO A VDU USER'S POSTURE CAN OFTEN IMPROVE THEIR OVERALL COMFORT. MANY EMPLOYERS SHOULD BE ABLE TO IDENTIFY SIMPLE SOLUTIONS - SUCH AS CHANGING THE USER'S POSTURE - AS A RESULT OF RISK ASSESSMENTS CARRIED OUT UNDER THE HEALTH AND SAFETY (DISPLAY SCREEN EQUIPMENT) REGULATIONS 1992.

GOOD SEATED POSTURE IS IMPORTANT IN MANY JOBS, EG FOR SUPERMARKET CASHIERS AND STAFF IN BANKS AND BUILDING SOCIETIES.

Before   After

TASK The commissioning editor in an editorial department of a national newspaper works on a VDU most of the working day. She uses the system to write to contributors, sub-edit copy, and to write her own material.

PROBLEM After a few months in this job (she had been a less intensive keyboard user in her last job), she developed aches and pains in her neck and back. To reduce the discomfort, she raised her height-adjustable chair until she was sitting with the keyboard at about elbow height. She could keep her wrists straight, with her arms hanging comfortably down from her shoulders. But she now developed discomfort in her lower back and legs, including pins and needles.

ASSESSING THE RISKS AND FINDING SOLUTIONS She went to the newspaper's ergonomics consultant for advice. Although she had improved her upper body posture by raising the chair, and reduced the pains in her neck and back, she couldn't now rest her feet on the floor. Her legs were unsupported. This put increased pressure on the underside of her thighs, reduced blood circulation and generally made her tense.

   The solution was a simple footrest. This was constructed in-house at almost no cost by the maintenance department using blockboard covered with an offcut of carpet.

RESULTS The footrest in effect raised the floor height so her legs were supported. It eliminated the lower back discomfort and pins and needles. Having raised her feet, she was able to find a more comfortable position by resting some of her body weight on the backrest.

ASSEMBLY WORK WHILE STANDING

TASK At a car interiors assembly plant most workstations were provided with thin rubber floor mats. They were intended to relieve some of the pressure on feet, knees and ankles which can result from standing or walking on hard surfaces.

PROBLEM Several employees reported symptoms of fatigue and soreness in their legs and lower back which they partly blamed on the thin mats not providing enough cushioning. Some employees tried to increase the cushioning by standing on folded cardboard boxes.

ASSESSING THE RISKS AND FINDING SOLUTIONS The rubber mats did provide some relief for employees who stood at their workstations, but they were too thin to be fully effective.

Before

The company investigated anti-fatigue mats and selected a brand to use throughout the plant that had a high foam density and a sloped edge to minimise trip hazards. They phased in the new mats by purchasing ten a month at a cost of £600 a month.

RESULTS The new anti-fatigue mats were welcomed by the employees, and reports of lower limb fatigue and discomfort have been eliminated.

After

Lower back
Legs

Awkward posture

Workstation design

JOBS WHICH INVOLVE STANDING IN ONE PLACE FOR LONG PERIODS OF TIME CAN LEAD TO FATIGUE AND DISCOMFORT IN THE LEGS AND BACK. A SOFTER SURFACE FOR EMPLOYEES TO STAND ON CAN REDUCE THESE SYMPTOMS. LOOK OUT FOR TELL-TALE SIGNS OF EMPLOYEE DISCOMFORT. MAKESHIFT WORKSTATION ADD-ONS, SUCH AS STANDING ON CARDBOARD, CAN OFTEN HIGHLIGHT PROBLEM AREAS EVEN IF THERE ARE NO FORMAL COMPLAINTS. EXTRA CUSHIONS, AND SITTING ON CARDBOARD, ARE COMMON SIGNS.

Hand

*Grip
Applied force*

Tool design

IT IS IMPORTANT TO AVOID NERVE DAMAGE TO THE HAND AND WRIST. PROLONGED EXPOSURE TO DIRECT PRESSURE ON THE NERVES IN THE HAND CAN CAUSE PAINFUL UPPER LIMB DISORDER SYMPTOMS. VERY OFTEN CUSHIONED GRIPS ON HANDTOOLS SIGNIFICANTLY REDUCE THE PRESSURE. THIS IS APPLICABLE TO ANY TASK WHERE HANDTOOLS ARE USED.

TASK   At a car interiors assembly plant operators used a tool to clean foam-filled padded instrument panels. The tool was angled and had a sharp point to pick out the excess foam around the edge of the panel.

Before

PROBLEM   Several operators complained about pain in their hands which they associated with using the tool.

ASSESSING THE RISKS AND FINDING SOLUTIONS   The tool had a 25 mm diameter wooden handle which most operators found too small to hold comfortably. Some had tried to fatten the handle by wrapping it with foam and tape. Wooden handles put direct pressure on the nerves running

After

through the centre of the hand, especially when gripped tightly or awkwardly. Here the problem was made worse by the short length of the handle, which pressed into the sensitive area at the base of the hand. The smooth surface of the wood made operators grip the tool more tightly, increasing the risk of upper limb disorders.

New wooden handles that were 50 mm in diameter were trialled, but the operators also found these uncomfortable.

The company researched the handles available for the tool, and finally selected a padded grip with a 38 mm diameter. Three were purchased at £60 each. A slight contour and padding reduced slippage in the hand, and the longer length reduced the direct pressure on the nerve running through the centre of the hand.

RESULTS   The operators said the new handles were much better. Reports of hand and wrist pain have reduced by 25%.

TASK   At a car manufacturing plant several operations called for the use of large powered tools, such as portable spot welders, which the operator held at the handles.   The handles were metal, roughly rectangular in cross-section, with a trigger pressed by two fingers to activate the tool.

PROBLEM   Several operators complained of aches to their hands which they blamed on the design of the tool. Fifty per cent of staff complained of 'trigger finger' to some degree. There had been lost time and changes to other work. Many operators had asked for a trigger which could be operated with the thumb.

ASSESSING THE RISKS AND FINDING SOLUTIONS   The design of the tool handle made it difficult to hold and control the spot welder and to activate the trigger. To activate the tool with the ends of the fingers, operators had to hold the handle in a pinching type grip between thumb and fingertips. The pressure applied to hold and control the tools was concentrated on the thumb and fingertips because they could not wrap their entire hand around the handle and have effective control over the trigger. Because of the small gripping surface, operators had to apply more force with their hands to grip the handles than if they had had a larger surface to hold.

One operator who regularly used these tools did research to find out what his colleagues disliked most about the current handle, and made prototype models using tools and materials within the plant. The new design had a number of improvements:
- the handle is wider and more rounded, with a slightly curved contour to fit comfortably into the operators' hands for improved grip;

- a thumb trigger was added to allow operators to wrap their entire hand around the handle when gripping it, and use the thumb to activate the tool. The old two finger trigger was kept in the new design for those who preferred it;
- an articulated flexi-joint was added at the interface between the handle and the tool to allow the handle to be moved to the most comfortable position;
- the handle end was made wider to keep the hand from slipping off.

The company spent around £2000 to get moulds made for casting the handles in its own foundry using scrap aluminium. Electrical work was carried out by the in-house maintenance team. The total estimated cost for development was around £5000.

RESULTS   The new handle is still at the prototype stage but has been on trial with several employees who find it much more comfortable to hold and use.

Hand

Grip
Applied force

Tool design

POOR HANDLE DESIGNS CAN REQUIRE TOO MUCH FORCE BY THE OPERATOR AND CREATE UNCOMFORTABLY HIGH PRESSURE ON THE AREAS OF THE HAND IN CONTACT WITH THE HANDLE. INVOLVING OPERATORS IN DESIGNING TOOLS AND PROVIDING FEEDBACK IS CRITICALLY IMPORTANT.

CUTTING DENIM USING A POWERED CUTTER

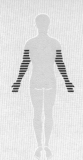

Upper limb

Force
Awkward posture

Tool design

HANDLES SHOULD BE DESIGNED TO GIVE MAXIMUM MECHANICAL ADVANTAGE, ESPECIALLY WHEN A LOT OF FORCE IS NEEDED. THE DESIGN OF THE HANDLE SHOULD ALLOW THE TOOL TO BE USED WHILE THE WRIST IS STRAIGHT. GOOD HANDLE DESIGN CAN LEAD TO MORE COMFORTABLE HAND POSITIONS, LESS FORCE, AND REDUCE THE RISK OF UPPER LIMB PROBLEMS.

TASK Denim cloth for jeans was cut into the right shapes using a powered cutter with a vertical blade. Staff cut through 120 ply of denim with a template as a guide.

PROBLEM One worker had developed an abrasion on the palm of his hand where he had been pushing on the end of the cutter handle.

ASSESSING THE RISKS AND FINDING SOLUTIONS A lot of force was needed to cut through the 120 ply material. It was made more difficult because the handle on the cutter was at a right angle to the blade, so staff had to work with their wrists bent. It was uncomfortable, and could cause upper limb disorders.

The company's Technology Centre designed a new handle, padded and curved to fit the hand for a better grip. It was adjustable and could be angled slightly downwards so the user's wrist was straight when applying force to push the cutter. The shape of the handle spread the pressure across the user's palm. The new handles fitted easily and cheaply to the existing cutters.

RESULTS Workers found the new handle more comfortable and easier to use. They could adjust the angle of the handle easily to get the most comfortable position. The worker's palm abrasion healed. The new handle gave the same level of accuracy, while reducing wrist strain and the risk of upper limb disorders.

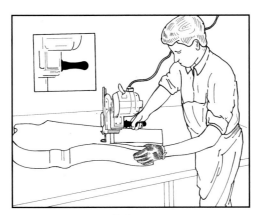

Before

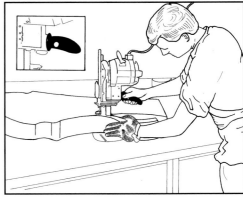

After

WORK AT A SUPERMARKET DELICATESSEN COUNTER

TASK Full-time supermarket staff served customers from behind a delicatessen counter. Merchandise was taken from the storage compartment in the counter, cut, weighed, priced, and packed by the staff and handed to the customer.

PROBLEM The company's hazard surveillance and referral system showed that ergonomic aspects of these counters needed improvement. A number of cases of injury to necks, lower backs, arms, shoulders and upper legs were identified.

ASSESSING THE RISKS AND FINDING SOLUTIONS The main risks came from repetitive and awkward reaching and stretching to take merchandise from the counter and pass it to the customers. In particular:

- cutting boards on runners along the back of the counter were made to slide out of the way and give easier reach, but in practice staff didn't move them;
- the height of the shelving at the back of the storage compartment meant staff had to reach over and in to get to merchandise;
- presentation was determined by selling considerations, so for example large hams were placed at the front before Christmas. Handling these put a lot of strain on the back, shoulders, and arms because of the stretching and the weight of the ham.

A number of solutions were introduced:

- in the short term, longer tongs were given to staff to cut the amount of reaching;
- the counter dressing strategy was changed to stop heavy or bulky items being put too far away from staff;
- the in-house training programme and written procedures were changed to emphasise good working practice, such as reducing reach by sliding the cutting boards out of the way;
- the next phase of counters were designed using more ergonomic information. Staff were consulted to help identify postural, maintenance, hygiene, and merchandising factors. Serving staff, occupational health specialists, section managers, personnel and marketing managers were involved, and refrigeration and food hygiene aspects were also considered, to provide good solutions.

RESULTS The new system has not been in operation very long, but the thorough design criteria should reduce risk of injury, increase productivity, and staff awareness and motivation.

Neck   Arm   Shoulder
Lower back
Lower legs

Awkward posture

Tool design
Task design
Workstation design

CONSULTING STAFF ABOUT PROBLEMS AND SOLUTIONS IS IMPORTANT. IT HELPS IDENTIFY ALL THE PROBLEMS, AND LEAD TO SOLUTIONS THAT ARE WORKABLE AND WILL BE USED BY STAFF.

PNEUMATIC STAPLING TASK

Shoulder

Awkward posture
Applied force

Tool design

TASK At a communications cabling manufacturing plant an operator used a hand-held pistol shaped stapling gun to attach wooden battens to the outside of cable reels. The operator held the 4 kg gun with one hand and drove staples into the sides of the reels between knee and eye level. Depending on the number of reels ordered, the operator could do this task for several hours each day.

PROBLEM Several operators reported fatigue and discomfort in the shoulder area which they associated with holding the heavy gun for long periods. The task probably contributed to sickness absence which operators took because of these pains.

ASSESSING THE RISKS AND FINDING SOLUTIONS To reduce the weight of the gun, a suspension system was provided. The staple gun was held on an inertial balance system suspended on a cantilever arm above the workstation. As it held most of the weight of the gun, the operator had only to move it to the various points on the side of the reel. The new system cost about £3000 to purchase and install.

RESULTS The numbers of complaints of upper limb fatigue and soreness have dropped.

Before

After

44

MICROSCOPE USE IN LABORATORIES

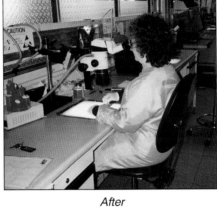

Before	*After*

TASK Operators at a computer manufacturing firm used microscopes to inspect printed circuit boards and other electronic components. Most operators worked at the microscopes for the entire day.

PROBLEM Some operators reported back and shoulder pain which they attributed to the work.

ASSESSING THE RISKS AND FINDING SOLUTIONS Because of the microscope design, many operators worked leaning forward with their heads tilted downwards to see into them. Holding this uncomfortable position for long periods of time was tiring and likely to cause musculoskeletal injury to the back and shoulders.

The employer decided that if the eyepiece was more adjustable, and so nearer the operator, they could sit in a more upright position to use it. The employer asked for this feature in the specification for new microscopes.

RESULTS The operators prefer the new microscopes and can work in a more comfortable position, reducing the risk of injury. The new microscopes were £3000 more expensive, but the employer judged that the cost was outweighed by the reduced musculoskeletal risk and improved quality and productivity.

Shoulder
Back

Awkward posture

Tool design

INTENSIVE TELEPHONE AND KEYBOARD USE

Neck
Shoulder

Awkward posture
Repetition

Tool design

THE HUNCHED NECK POSTURE OF VDU USERS TALKING ON THE TELEPHONE IS A COMMON SIGHT IN THE MODERN OFFICE. IF THE INDIVIDUAL'S JOB NORMALLY INVOLVES A LARGE AMOUNT OF SIMULTANEOUS TELEPHONE AND VDU USE, EG IN TELESALES AND SALES DEPARTMENTS, A HEADPHONE DEVICE IS AN EASY WAY TO REDUCE DISCOMFORT AND THE RISK OF NECK INJURY.

TASK The consumer affairs correspondent of a daily newspaper spends much of his time investigating stories and collecting information by telephone while making notes on his VDU. He then uses the VDU system to write and edit his own copy.

PROBLEM Working to a tight daily schedule, he often worked for long periods with the phone receiver jammed in his neck by hunching his shoulder. Gripping the receiver this way caused a lot of tension and discomfort in his neck and shoulder.

ASSESSING THE RISKS AND FINDING SOLUTIONS He got a sponge rubber gadget to help stop the telephone from slipping, but considerable tension was still needed to keep it in place. The discomfort remained, so he went to the newspaper's ergonomics consultant for advice.

To remove the tension altogether, the telephone hand set was replaced by a headset with earphones and a microphone which could be worn comfortably for long periods and meant the correspondent could use the keyboard or pen and paper normally. The headset plugged into the telephone receiver and cost about £20.

Before

RESULTS The journalist was able to carry out telephone interviews and type his notes directly into the VDU without undue strain. The headset was light and having two ear pieces made it easier to hear and therefore concentrate on the content of the interview without distraction in a noisy newsroom. His discomfort disappeared.

After

VEHICLE TRIM-CUTTING

TASK In the production of custom vehicles, the plastic protective trim for the roof, doors etc is hand cut to individual lengths.

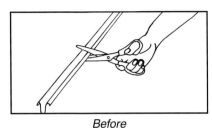
Before

PROBLEM An operator in the trim department reported finger and hand discomfort to the company's occupational health unit, and was diagnosed with tendonitis.

After

ASSESSING THE RISKS AND FINDING SOLUTIONS The operator's task was assessed. Although shears were available, she was found to be using scissors to cut the trim. She cut about 100 pieces an hour, in up to two-hour stretches. The scissors were clearly wrong for the task. Because of the thickness of the trim, they had to be gripped very hard to cut it. The operator was moved into other work that didn't involve intensive use of her hands for long periods. Management made sure that other operators were using the right tools.

RESULTS Unfortunately the original operator still suffers discomfort, although she no longer does hand-intensive tasks, and may need surgery to ease the problem.

Shears are a much better tool for the task, as they do not need such a forceful grip and are regularly sharpened. By making sure other staff use them, the company is reducing the risk of other problems. But to reduce the risk still further, the company will introduce guillotines, removing altogether the need for forceful and repetitive gripping.

Hand

Grip
Applied force
Repetition

Tool design
Individual organisation

It is not always easy to make sure that people use the right tools for a task. This study shows what can happen if the wrong ones are used. This problem only came to the company's attention when the operator already had a lot of discomfort. Initial staff training on how to use the right tools, continual checks by management and colleagues, and encouraging staff to report problems early, should be emphasised and re-emphasised as part of every organisation's health and safety procedures.

Shoulder

Awkward posture
Applied force

Tool design

TASK Operators at an engine company used a powered nut runner to assemble the engine front cover, gear and flywheel housing. The operator drove over 2000 nuts on a typical shift. The nuts had to be driven to a critical level of torque to meet the company's manufacturing standards. When the nut running tool reached the desired level of torque, it would shut off immediately.

PROBLEM All operators complained about the 'kick' caused by the recoil of the nut runner after the nut was driven and 20% reported pain. One operator had suffered a serious shoulder injury when the tool failed to shut off and the torque was transferred to his arm. It resulted in a £2000 compensation claim and the cost of several weeks' absence.

ASSESSING THE RISKS AND FINDING SOLUTIONS The sudden stress on the hand and wrist caused by the kickback when the tool shut off, combined with the frequency of the task and the postures required, presented a risk of upper limb disorder to the 30 team members who performed the task.

A variable torque tool was introduced to replace the old nut runner. This had a clutch mechanism which automatically altered the effective torque as the right level of tightening was reached, and gradually shut off the tool. There was no sudden kickback once the nut was fastened. Each new nut running tool cost about £8000 for the gun and the electric controller. It was introduced with other planned changes to the production system.

RESULTS The operators found the new tools far more comfortable to use. There have been no complaints of pain in the eighteen months since they were introduced and the company has specified them as standard.

NUT RUNNING IS COMMON IN MANUFACTURING/ASSEMBLY TASKS IN A WIDE VARIETY OF INDUSTRIES. THE PROPER SELECTION OF TOOLS CAN HAVE A DRAMATIC EFFECT ON USERS' OVERALL COMFORT AND IN TURN THE NUMBER OF MUSCULOSKELETAL PROBLEMS THEY HAVE. WHEN SELECTING TOOLS, CONSIDER WHETHER THERE ARE ANY UNDESIRABLE FEATURES THAT COULD REDUCE THE EFFECTIVENESS OF THE TOOL AND HARM OPERATORS.

MANIFOLD ASSEMBLY

Hand

TASK   Manifolds are used in the manufacture of domestic gas cookers. To manufacture the manifold an operator held up to eight manifolds in her left hand, started the screws off manually, and then tightened them with a manual screwdriver. She assembled about 50 manifolds an hour.

PROBLEM   The operator who did this task on a regular basis began to suffer from discomfort in both her right and left hands. She was diagnosed with tenosynovitis in her right hand, and carpal tunnel syndrome in her left. She was off work for four months with these injuries.

Awkward posture
Repetition
Applied force

Tool design
Workstation design

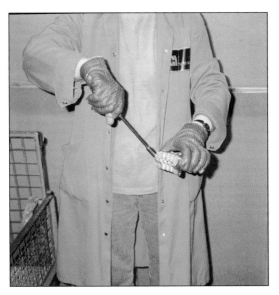

Before

After

ASSESSING THE RISKS AND FINDING SOLUTIONS   The site occupational health nurse wanted to minimise the problematic hand stretching and twisting movements associated with the task. A rig to hold the manifolds tightly was built out of wood, and a torque-controlled air screwdriver was purchased to twist the screws into the manifold. The operator now has only to start the screws by hand and push the rig along under the screwdriver. The changes cost £500.

RESULTS
- Much less manual force is required to complete the operation and the task is easier and more comfortable.
- The risk of injury to both hands has been greatly reduced.
- There is less wastage of material, as the screw threads are less likely to become blunted.
- The quality of the finished product has improved.

MANY ASSEMBLY OPERATIONS IN ENGINEERING COMPANIES REQUIRE COMPONENTS TO BE SCREWED INTO PLACE. THIS TYPE OF OPERATION, WHEN PERFORMED MANUALLY WITH HIGH RATES OF REPETITION, IS VERY LIKELY TO LEAD TO DISCOMFORT IN THE HAND AND WRIST. THE BEST WAY TO DEAL WITH THE RISK IS TO REDUCE OR REMOVE THE MANUAL TWISTING. BENEFITS CAN INCLUDE LESS WASTAGE AND BETTER PRODUCT QUALITY AS WELL AS REDUCED RISKS TO HEALTH.

REMOVING UNWANTED THREADS FROM JEANS

Upper limb

Applied force
Repetition
Grip

Tool design

ALL TOOLS SHOULD BE DESIGNED TO BE FIT FOR THEIR PURPOSE. HANDLES SHOULD BE LARGE ENOUGH TO BE USED COMFORTABLY. AS WELL AS EASING THE STRAIN ON THE HAND AND FINGER MUSCLES, GOOD HANDLES MAKE TOOLS EASIER TO CONTROL, AND SO REDUCE THE RISK OF ACCIDENTS.

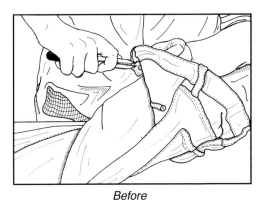

Before

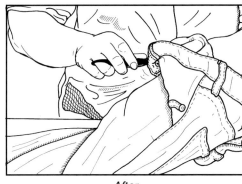

After

TASK In the inspection and finishing stage of jeans manufacture, any excess threads are trimmed from the garment using small snips.

PROBLEM The snips were uncomfortable to use and a number of accidents had been reported where the user's hand had slipped over the blade. The snips had to be sharpened up to three times a day by engineering staff, and employees often used blunt snips as they waited for sharpening.

ASSESSING THE RISKS AND FINDING SOLUTIONS The snips were uncomfortable because of the strain on the fingers which were pushed into the backs of the blades without enough protection or cushioning. The lack of adequate handles made the snips more difficult to use, and coupled with the force needed to use the blunt snips, made the development of upper limb disorders a possibility.

The Purchasing Department got new disposable snips. After a number of different types were tried, a suitable design was found with a thumb pad and plastic finger guard.

RESULTS The new snips were easier to use, more comfortable to grasp, and the workforce preferred them. Because they were disposable, fresh snips could be used instead of waiting to have them sharpened, and so work was always done with sharp blades. There was a saving in engineers' time as they did not need to sharpen the snips. With sharper blades, less force was needed to cut the loose threads. There were fewer accidents as the thumb pad and finger hold prevented the hand from slipping down the blade and the risk of upper limb injuries was reduced. Product quality also improved with the constant use of sharp blades.

50

TASK Operators at a helicopter manufacturing plant used a ratchet spanner to turn and screw a 'rosean' (a steel peg threaded at both ends) into a transmission housing. An operator had to insert between 87 and 108 roseans into each transmission, and the whole housing unit took one employee over eight hours to assemble.

PROBLEM Several operators reported elbow and upper arm pains which they associated with the task.

ASSESSING THE RISKS AND FINDING SOLUTIONS The repetitive motion required to turn the spanner, combined with poor arm posture and large forces, presented a risk of upper limb disorders.

Pneumatic nut runners were introduced. They would have cost less than £130, but were already available in house. The tool allowed the operator to turn the rosean to screw it into the transmission housing simply by squeezing a trigger rather than repeatedly turning the ratchet spanner.

Elbow
Upper arm

Repetition
Awkward posture
Applied force

Tool design

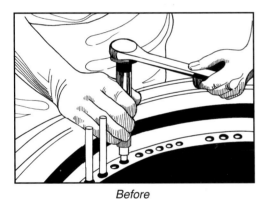

Before

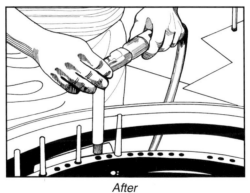

After

RESULTS

- A reduction in reports of upper limb pains.
- The unit assembly time was cut from eight hours to five hours.
- The product quality improved with a lower rejection rate on inspection of the driven roseans.

APPLICATION OF TORQUES

Elbow
Back
Shoulder

Applied force

Tool design

THE APPLICATION OF TORQUE IS COMMON IN MANY MANUFACTURING OPERATIONS WHERE PARTS MUST BE TIGHTENED OR LOOSENED. A MECHANICAL AID LIKE A TORQUE MULTIPLIER CAN REDUCE THE AMOUNT OF TORQUE APPLIED BY THE OPERATOR AND REDUCE INJURIES.

TASK Operators at a helicopter manufacturing plant used a torqueing device to install a bearing into a spindle sleeve assembly used on the rotor head. They placed a torquing tool weighing 25 kg in the centre of the assembly, attached a pair of long bars to the device, and two men input about 600 ft/lbs of torque to line up the components and complete the installation. If they did not get the proper line up of components, the job needed four men to 'break' the seal with 2600 ft/lbs of torque and reposition and repeat the installation.

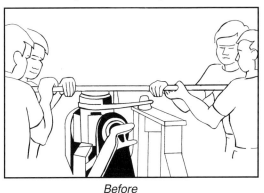

Before   After

PROBLEM Over time, some operators suffered elbow, shoulder and back injuries.

ASSESSING THE RISKS AND FINDING SOLUTIONS

Hazard/risk	*Solution*
The high forces required by the operator applying torque created stress to the upper limbs.	A new torque multiplier tool was was devised for about £800, which reduced the force applied by the operator to 90 ft/lbs. The remaining torque was applied by the multiplier.
The heavy weight of the torquing tool presented a risk of injury to the back or shoulders.	The new tool weighed only 6 kg, reducing the risk of manual handling injury.

RESULTS Injuries in this area have reduced by 75%. The modified method also reduced the working hours on the job by about 50% and rework was significantly reduced.

CLIP INSTALLATION

TASK Three operators at a car interiors manufacturing plant installed clips to secure instrument panels to brackets at a standing workstation. The clips are fixed at attachment points where screws will be used for other components.

PROBLEM One operator complained of pain around her shoulder which she attributed to reaching upwards to the fixed work height.

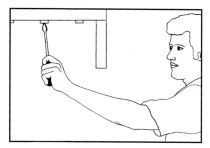

Before

ASSESSING THE RISKS AND FINDING SOLUTIONS Reaching up above shoulder height - an awkward posture - caused shoulder soreness and could cause upper limb disorders. The risk was greater for shorter operators who had to reach further. An adjustable mounting bracket was devised in-house, which allowed each employee to adjust the workstation easily to meet their needs and work without stretching.

It was noticed that when installing clips the operators had to repeatedly bend back their wrists. This awkward and repetitive movement suggested that wrist injuries were possible. A modified screwdriver was devised to help install the clips. This tool reduced the awkward wrist movement.

The total cost of these changes was £20.

After

RESULTS The operator's symptoms of shoulder pain have been eliminated. The overall number of complaints and injuries associated with this task have also reduced since the changes.

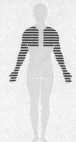

Shoulder
Upper limb

Awkward posture

Tool design
Workstation design

MAKING WORKSTATIONS ADJUSTABLE TO IMPROVE OPERATOR POSTURE AND PROVIDING PROPER TOOLS FOR THE TASK ARE IMPORTANT MEASURES THROUGHOUT INDUSTRY TO HELP PREVENT AND REDUCE ALL MUSCULOSKELETAL PROBLEMS.

Hand
Wrist

Repetition
Grip
Applied force

Supporting clamp/jig
Component selection

MANUALLY INTENSIVE ASSEMBLY TASKS LIKE THIS ARE FOUND IN SEVERAL INDUSTRIES, INCLUDING ELECTRONICS. IN MANUALLY INTENSIVE JOBS, THE OPERATOR'S POSTURE, USE OF FORCE AND REPETITION OF THE TASK CAN LEAD TO DISCOMFORT AND INJURY. MECHANICAL AIDS CAN REDUCE THE PHYSICAL STRESS OF MANUAL TASKS AND SO THE RISK OF INJURY. ORDERING PARTS PRE-CUT TO THE PROPER SIZE ELIMINATES THE NEED FOR OPERATOR CUTTING - OFTEN A REPETITIVE TASK.

TASK Operators at a jewellery manufacturing plant assembled button clusters. They:

- took a pre-assembled cluster from the pile and held it in the left hand;
- grasped the wires from the bottom of the cluster using a pair of needle nose pliers;
- twisted the wires by turning both hands in opposite directions, 12 to 15 times;
- placed the completed cluster in another pile.

The operator also had to cut the wires and springs for the buttons to the proper length. The operator did this all day, assembling one cluster every 20 seconds.

PROBLEM Several operators complained of hand and wrist pain, although there were no officially reported injuries associated with the job. One operator was taken off the job because of pain in her wrists.

ASSESSING THE RISKS AND FINDING SOLUTIONS The repetitive wrist twisting and gripping forces needed to hold the button cluster and pliers presented a risk of wrist injury. Operators also risked shoulder injury from holding their arms up unsupported while twisting the wires.

A fixture was developed which held the cluster in a clamp and removed the need for the operator to twist the wire. A tool was also developed to cut the wire to length, and springs for the buttons were ordered cut to size, so no hand cutting was required.

The total material and labour cost of the modifications was about £240.

RESULTS

- The operators' hand and wrist postures were improved and the injured worker was able to return to work without symptoms of soreness.
- The productivity rate increased by 70%.
- Quality improved as product variation was eliminated.

HEART VALVE CONSTRUCTION

TASK   Operators in a medical supplies company prepared replacement human heart valves using pig hearts. Quality control checks included tying off two arteries in the hearts before testing the valves for leaks. This was done by holding the pig heart in one hand, and pinching the ends of the arteries closed with the fingers of that hand. The operator then wrapped a string around the artery, tied a knot and cut off the spare string with scissors. This was repeated on the other artery.

Each operator did this eight hours a day, tying off 1000 arteries on 500 pig hearts.

PROBLEM   Some operators reported discomfort and cramps in their hands. A job rotation scheme was introduced so that each operator did the task only two days each week. The pains reduced but still remained. It was agreed that a change in the task was needed to reduce the risk of long-term hand and wrist injuries.

Before

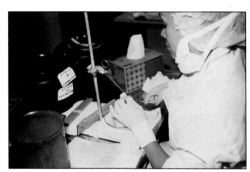

After

ASSESSING THE RISKS AND FINDING SOLUTIONS   Several risk factors were identified:

- the awkward and fixed position (static posture) of the hand holding the heart;
- a lot of pinching force on the artery ends;
- highly repetitive actions in both hands.

A holding fixture of forceps attached to a base in front of the operator was made in house for about £12. The forceps opened and closed by moving the free end of the forceps grip. The operator closed the forceps on the end of the artery, which pinched it shut and suspended the heart. The strings around the artery were then tied and cut as before, but without the heart being held in the hand.

RESULTS   The risk of an upper limb disorder building up was reduced when the risk factors were removed. The operators said they were far more comfortable and reports of hand and wrist pain stopped. Productivity increased by 50%.

Hand

Awkward posture
Grip   Applied force
Repetition

Supporting clamp/jig
Task design

USING THE HAND AS A 'BIOLOGICAL CLAMP' IS COMMON AND OFTEN UNNECESSARY IN ASSEMBLY TASKS. HOLDING THE HAND IN A FIXED AND STILL POSITION OFTEN LEADS TO MUSCLE FATIGUE AND ACHES. THIS CAN DEVELOP INTO A MORE SERIOUS DISORDER, PARTICULARLY IF A HARD GRIP IS USED AS WELL. IN THIS CASE A MECHANICAL CLAMP HAS AVOIDED POOR HAND POSTURE AND GRIPPING.

DATE-MAKER SUB-ASSEMBLY OPERATIONS

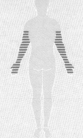

Upper limb

*Applied force
Awkward posture
Grip*

*Supporting clamp/jig
Workstation design*

THIS STUDY SHOWS HOW FAIRLY SIMPLE CHANGES TO WORKSTATION DESIGN CAN HAVE A BIG IMPACT ON THE WORKER'S POSTURE AND COMFORT. IN THIS TYPE OF FINE ASSEMBLY TASK, USING A JIG OR FIXTURE TO HOLD A PART REMOVES THE NEED FOR THE WORKER TO HOLD IT. AS WELL AS REDUCING RISK, THIS OFTEN RESULTS IN IMPROVED PRODUCTIVITY AND A MORE COMFORTABLE WORKER.

TASK The assembly line for the manufacture of franking machines had a central assembly line with feeder lines supplying sub-assembled components. The main tasks in the sub-assembly of the machine's date-maker included:

- picking up the first bracket and placing it onto the clamp;
- placing a plastic cog onto the first bracket;
- building up another plastic cog;
- putting the cogs together;
- locating the metal date cog onto the plastic cogs;
- locating pins into holes;
- banging in pins;
- zeroing the date.

There were 12 separate components that made up the date-maker dials which were assembled at a rate of 38 per hour.

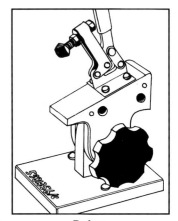

Before

PROBLEM Workers reported painful pressure around the wrist, and upper limb disorders. There was also worker absenteeism.

ASSESSING THE RISKS AND FINDING SOLUTIONS A number of risks were identified including:

After

- left hand used as a clamp to hold cogs steady while they were built;
- wrists bent too far up;
- worker sitting too low, so raising elbow and shoulder awkwardly;
- one arm held behind body to bang pins into dial because hammer handle was too long;
- resting wrists on sharp edge of metal block, causing pressure to build up and restricting blood flow.

To reduce these risks, changes were made to the task:

- a new jig design was introduced with an inset fitting to hold the dial. This made a steady point to work from and meant the left hand was used less as a clamp, and wrists were in a straighter position;
- the metal block was lowered, so elbows and shoulders were lowered to a comfortable position;
- the edges of the block were rounded off;
- high-backed adjustable chairs and adjustable footrests were introduced to improve overall posture;
- because the job was particularly hand intensive, regular breaks were taken in the shift and more job rotation was introduced to include less hand intensive tasks.

RESULTS There were no further reports of painful pressure around the wrists, no more reports of upper limb disorders, and worker absenteeism reduced 100%.

TYRE SEQUENCING

TASK Van tyres are delivered into a tyre bay stacked upright in racks, two high. They are then loaded onto a conveyor belt to be delivered to other parts of the factory. The tyres are taken off the racks and placed flat, in stacks up to seven tyres high, in the loading area, then lifted in the flat position onto the conveyor. On average, two tyres per minute were placed on the conveyor from the flat position.

PROBLEM Operators risked upper limb and back injuries.

ASSESSING THE RISKS AND FINDING SOLUTIONS A risk assessment showed that the width of the tyres made gripping them difficult. Lifting the tyres from the floor to the conveyor required the operator to use both hands, and stretch to place them on the conveyor. The weight of the tyres, at 27 kg, was identified as risky for a one-person lift.

The health and safety manager for the site wanted to remove the need for handling, to avoid the risk of injury, but the change had to be achieved at no cost.

The part of the operation requiring the tyres to be stacked flat was removed. Instead, they were rolled off the delivery rack, and leant in the upright position against the wall in the loading area. Secondly, a metal ramp was made so the operator rolled the upright tyre onto the conveyor. When on the conveyor, the tyre was lowered into the flat position.

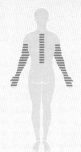

Upper limb
Back

Manual handling

Task design
Workstation design

In many industries, loading and unloading of products onto conveyors poses a risk to staff. Simple modifications to loading areas, such as the ramp used here, provide cheap but effective solutions to remove risk.

Before

After

RESULTS With the new loading method, and the ramp, the lifting and stretching problems were removed.

- The operators find the task more comfortable and much less tiring.
- The risk of back injury has been reduced, as all the weight is taken by the floor and the ramp, not by the operator. The weight lifted has dropped from 27 kg to 9 kg (max).
- The time taken to complete the task has reduced.

REPLACING COAL ONTO A CONVEYOR BELT

Back

Awkward posture
Manual handling

![tick]

Task design
Machinery design

PLASTIC SHEETING, OR OTHER 'GUTTERING' CAN BE USED TO COLLECT RAW MATERIALS FALLING FROM A CONVEYOR. OFTEN LOADS CAN BE MOVED WITHOUT BEING LIFTED MANUALLY - MECHANICAL MEANS CAN REMOVE THE RISK OF INJURY. EFFORTS SHOULD BE MADE TO REDUCE THE NUMBER OF TIMES A LOAD IS HANDLED.

TASK Coal was transported on a sloped conveyor belt from a storage area into a power station. Large quantities of coal fell off the belt, and so operatives at the bottom had to shovel it from floor level back onto the belt.

PROBLEM The operatives clearly risked back injuries. It was recognised that the process was inefficient and a poor use of manpower.

ASSESSING THE RISKS AND FINDING SOLUTIONS The operatives were working in bad postures - bending, stretching, and reaching awkwardly with heavy loads - to reach coal that sometimes fell in difficult places. It was often lifted on the shovel above head height as it was loaded onto the conveyor.

In-house engineering staff designed and implemented their own solution. Plastic sheeting was installed underneath the conveyor so that the fallen coal was washed down with water and collected at the bottom. The resulting slurry was pumped up and the water removed, before the coal was mechanically replaced onto the conveyor belt.

RESULTS A lot less manual handling was needed for the task, reducing the risk of injury. The more efficient use of manpower that the changes allowed provided scope for the redeployment of staff.

CASED BEER DISTRIBUTION

TASK   A large spirits producer sold its employees about 6500 cases of beer each year from its staff shop. The cases were delivered to a garage, and then moved 75 yards to the staff shop. The shop assistant had to lift each case sold from the back of the shop to the counter. The customers then had to carry them 50 to 100 yards to their parked cars.

PROBLEM   The shop assistants reported back pain linked to moving the cases.

ASSESSING THE RISKS AND FINDING SOLUTIONS   The system the company used meant that the same item was handled four times. The problem was worst for the assistants who repeatedly carried cases, but customers carrying cases the long distance to the car park also risked back injury.

A new system was introduced which reduced the number of times and distances the cases were carried. It cost nothing. The cases stayed in the garage where they were delivered. Customers paid for the beer at the shop and were given a voucher. Each Thursday they could drive to the garage, present their vouchers to the sales assistant, collect the beer and carry it a few yards to their cars.

RESULTS   The overall amount of handling was reduced and reports of back pain among shop assistants has decreased.

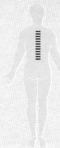

Back

*Manual handling
Repetition*

Task design

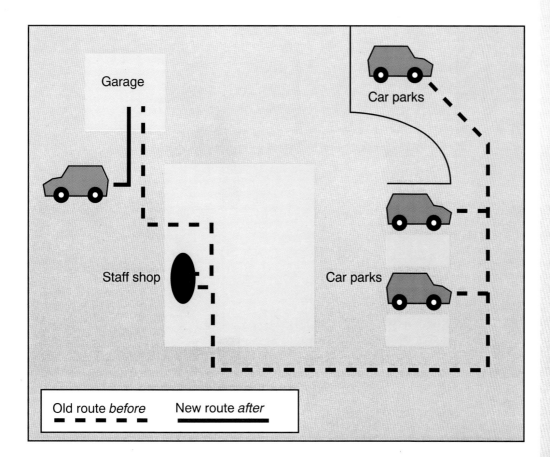

Garage

Car parks

Staff shop

Car parks

Old route *before*   New route *after*

WHEN ASSESSING MANUAL HANDLING TASKS, THINK FIRST IF IT IS POSSIBLE TO AVOID HANDLING THE LOAD. THE ORGANISATIONAL CHANGE IN THIS EXAMPLE MEANT MOST OF THE HANDLING HAD GONE. CHANGING THE WAY TASKS ARE ORGANISED OFTEN COSTS NOTHING, AND CAN HELP AVOID HANDLING.

PACKING LINEN BOXES

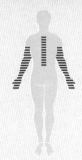

Back
Upper limb

Manual handling

Component design

THE SHAPE OF THE LOAD IN MANUAL HANDLING TASKS CAN AFFECT HOW EASY OR DIFFICULT SOMETHING IS TO LIFT. IF LOADS CAN BE REDESIGNED TO A MORE MANAGEABLE SHAPE, THE RISK OF INJURY CAN BE REDUCED. SOLVING A PROBLEM IN ONE DEPARTMENT CAN LEAD TO SIMILAR BENEFITS IN OTHER DEPARTMENTS, AND STANDARDISING CONTAINERS MAKES PURCHASING, STAFF TRAINING, AND STORAGE DESIGN EASIER AND CHEAPER.

TASK Staff in a hospital had to make up boxes of linen to order. The different items of linen were taken from shelves and loaded into cardboard boxes. The full boxes were loaded on a pallet for removal to an outer storage area. Over two hundred linen orders were made up in a day.

PROBLEM Staff were dissatisfied with this job because the boxes were large and hard to handle. Some staff with a history of back problems couldn't do it.

ASSESSING THE RISKS AND FINDING SOLUTIONS The box design, the repeated lifting and stacking, and the fact that staff had no prior knowledge of what each box weighed, put them at risk of back and upper limb injuries.

It was decided to reduce the dimensions of the boxes to make them lighter and easier to handle. The local manager sought the co-operation of other departments so that they could bulk buy the new size boxes. At the same time, a graph giving the weight of each of the standard orders was put on a nearby notice-board to alert staff to the weight of many of the boxes.

RESULTS
- Risk of manual handling injuries reduced with easier to handle boxes and knowledge of their weight.
- Number of staff complaints reduced.
- Staff flexibility improved.
- The new boxes could be used by other departments for purposes other than storing linen.

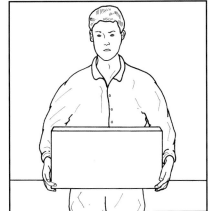

Before

After

PAPER TISSUE WINDING MACHINE OPERATION

TASK Operatives in a paper-mill loaded a tissue winding and slitting machine. They:

- put 15 empty cardboard cores onto a mandrel (a solid metal bar weighing 15 kg) which they held upright;
- lifted the mandrel to shoulder height and, reaching forward, inserted it into the machine;
- closed the machine guard and started the machine;
- removed the mandrel when the roll winding and slitting operation was completed;
- removed the rolls from the mandrel and repeated the process.

The operatives performed this cycle about once every four minutes.

Elbow
Back
Shoulder

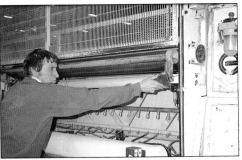

Before

After

Manual handling
Repetition

Component design

PROBLEM Some of the operatives reported elbow pain which they associated with this task.

ASSESSING THE RISKS AND FINDING SOLUTIONS Handling the mandrel was difficult because of its weight and length, and the height at which it had to be inserted into the machine. Holding it at shoulder height while trying to mount both ends into the right slots meant the operatives had to hold a difficult position for too long. This caused tiredness and stress to their shoulders and lower backs as well.

Putting the empty cardboard cores into the mandrel was a highly repetitive task. Each core had to be inserted over the end of the mandrel at shoulder height. This could contribute to tiredness or injury in the arm or shoulder.

The tissue winding machine was scheduled to be upgraded, and both the process and equipment were changed to reduce these problems. The mandrel was replaced with a lighter, single, cardboard core. Plastic lugs were put at the end of each core to mount it into the machine. It replaced the mandrel and the 15 empty cores. Once the machine had finished winding, the single core and the tissue was slit into 15 cores at another machine. These changes were integrated into a pre-planned upgrade of the machine line costing about £50 000.

The modified operation reduced risks by reducing the load and cutting out some of the repetitive movements.

RESULTS The improvement was made mainly to increase productivity, but since the change the operatives have found the job less demanding and there have been no reports of pain.

FABRIC ROLL SLITTING OPERATION

Hand
Wrist

Applied force
Repetition

Component design

Pin and groove locks can be used in many operations where materials are sorted and used on rolls, especially in the textile and paper industries. It is an example of a relatively inexpensive modification to a traditional method which eliminates the risk of injury, and can increase productivity.

TASK Operators in a luggage manufacturing plant placed a roll of material on a bar and locked the bar into a yoke. To lock it they had to twist a threaded knob against the metal bar. The operator twisted the knob 500 to 800 times each day, and performed the whole task about 15 times.

PROBLEM Operators found the task fatiguing.

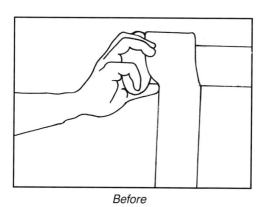

| Before | After |

ASSESSING THE RISKS AND FINDING SOLUTIONS The repeated twisting action needed to lock the bar could cause hand and wrist injuries over time, especially as a high force was needed to turn the knob.

The screw lock was replaced with an easy to use pin and groove lock. The operator simply inserted the pin so that it ran through the holes in the support yoke and the fabric roll bar. The change cost less than £60.

RESULTS The new method of locking the bar not only removed the problematic twisting actions, but was also faster. The time taken to lock the yoke reduced from eight seconds to two seconds. Operators found the new method much easier and less tiring.

PHOTOCOPIER MANUFACTURE

TASK Operators at a leading photocopier manufacturing firm manually moved fuser rolls (internal parts for the photocopier) from a trolley to a machine which applied a primary coat of paint. For quality reasons it was important that the operator did not touch the rolls, so they were mounted on a spindle through their centre and stored upright. The operator:

- lifted the roll by grasping the top of the spindle;
- mounted it into the machine;
- removed a painted roller;
- indexed the machine;
- repeated the task.

On a typical day an operator did this around 570 times, ie lifting the individual rollers, weighing 2.2 kg, over 1100 times.

PROBLEM One of the four operators reported pains in his arm and hands. The other operators were also found to have had similar symptoms of upper limb discomfort.

ASSESSING THE RISKS AND FINDING SOLUTIONS A team was assigned to assess the task and develop improvements. The problem was in the way the operator held the spindle, pinching it between the thumb and index finger. The top of the spindle was slightly knurled, but lifting the roll still required a high pinching force and awkward arm posture.

Changes were tested out in trials with the co-operation of the operators. The solution involved re-cutting the tops of the spindles, in-house, using a milling machine. The tops were further indented, in the shape and size to fit a man's thumb, so that the operators had a more secure grip when lifting them. This reduced the amount of pinching force they had to apply. It cost between £800 and £1000 to change 640 spindles.

RESULTS Operators report that the task is much easier with the improved spindle tops. The change was implemented over a year ago and there have been no complaints of upper limb discomfort since.

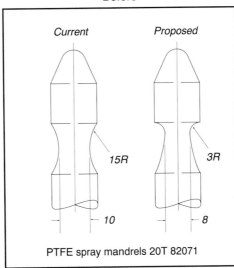

Before

Current   Proposed

15R   3R

10   8

PTFE spray mandrels 20T 82071

After

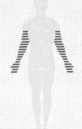

Upper limb

Awkward posture
Grip
Applied force

Component design

HIGH PINCH GRIP FORCES, ALONG WITH POOR WRIST POSTURES AND HIGH REPETITION, ARE A MAJOR CONTRIBUTOR TO UPPER LIMB INJURIES. CHANGING THE SHAPE OF THE OBJECT BEING GRASPED CAN REDUCE THE PINCHING FORCE AND THE RISK OF INJURY. OTHER PINCHING TASKS, SUCH AS GRASPING PARTS FOR ASSEMBLY, ARE COMMON IN THE ELECTRONICS, CAR, AEROSPACE AND OTHER INDUSTRIES.

GAMES PACKING OPERATION

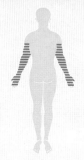

Upper limb

Awkward posture
Grip
Applied force

Component design
Task design
Workstation design

PACKING OPERATIONS ARE COMMON IN MOST MANUFACTURING INDUSTRIES. THEY ARE OFTEN VERY REPETITIVE AND PRESENT A RISK OF UPPER LIMB DISORDERS. A PROPER RISK ASSESSMENT AND MEASURES TO REDUCE THE RISKS CAN RESULT IN SIGNIFICANT DESIGN IMPROVEMENTS AND REDUCE INJURIES. IT MAY ALSO PROVIDE SUBSTANTIAL PRODUCTION BENEFITS.

TASK Operators at a games manufacturing plant packed board games into a corrugated master carton. The sequence of operations was as follows:

- games emerge from a high speed heat tunnel sealed with 'shrink wrap'. The operator lifts the game (weighing about 1.5 kg) from the delivery conveyor and inspects it for faulty wrap;
- if the wrap does not meet quality standards, the worker tells the heat tunnel operator and puts the defective product aside;
- acceptable games are packed horizontally, and one at a time, into a master carton, which is tilted towards the worker and supported by a roller conveyor 32 inches high;
- the operator packs six games into each carton, and usually has to force the last one in because of air trapped in the shrink wrap. This can damage the shrink wrap and the product;
- the full master carton is offloaded at another station.

PROBLEM About 9% of the upper limb disorders occurring in the plant arose from these packing operations.

ASSESSING THE RISKS AND FINDING SOLUTIONS Following training in ergonomics, the company engineers did a risk assessment. They found a number of risk factors:

- to pick up the game boxes from the delivery conveyor operators bent their right wrists in an awkward angle while gripping the box;
- hard (high force) pinching grips were needed to lift the boxes off the conveyor with one hand, and to push the last two boxes into the master carton;
- shoulder and back stress was caused by stooping and stretching to reach the game boxes on the delivery conveyor and the angle of the master carton.

Changes made to the workstation to reduce these risks included:

- raising the delivery conveyor from 32 inches to 37 inches;
- reducing the speed of the conveyor from 140 ft/min to 70 ft/min without reducing line throughput;
- repositioning the conveyor to reduce reaching distance from 17 inches to 11 inches;
- installing a 'packing table' on the end of the delivery conveyor allowing automatic stacking of boxes (two high) before pick up;
- establishing a work procedure to encourage stacking so the games are picked up in twos (hence reducing the number of turning movements);
- raising the roller conveyor for the master cartons;
- reducing the tilt of the master cartons for packing;
- fitting roller conveyors to help remove the full cartons;
- increasing the size of the shipping carton to ease packing.

These modifications cost about £1500 to implement.

Before

After

The new workstation was tested in production conditions and reassessed. This revealed that stress to the shoulders, back and right arm were significantly reduced as a result of eliminating most reaches and forward bending. Wrist postures also improved and the gripping forces were less. As well as reducing the risk of upper limb disorders, the new workstation resulted in a 90% reduction in damage to the packaging and related returns from customers.

SPRING BUNDLING

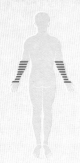

Wrist
Lower arm

Grip
Applied force
Repetition

Component design
Tool design

FOREARM TWISTING ACTIONS ARE COMMON ACROSS INDUSTRY, WHETHER IN DRIVING SCREWS OR TWISTING WIRES. SUCH REPETITIVE TWISTING OF THE FOREARM CAN LEAD TO 'TENNIS ELBOW' AND OTHER UPPER LIMB DISORDERS OVER TIME. AS THIS STUDY SHOWS, SOLUTIONS CAN BE FOUND WHICH REMOVE THE NEED TO ROTATE THE ARM, AND OFTEN IMPROVE JOB EFFICIENCY TOO.

TASK   Operators at a luggage manufacturing plant tied together bundles of machine-produced springs. They cut a length of wire, wrapped it around the spring bundle and used a pair of pliers to twist it together. Each wire took one strong grip to cut it, and five to ten twists to tighten it around a bundle. Each operator prepared about 160 bundles per shift.

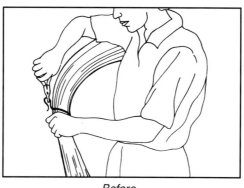

| Before | After |

PROBLEM   The operators found the task stressful on their wrists and forearms and several wore wrist bands because of the pain from the task. One had suffered an injury to his left wrist.

ASSESSING THE RISKS AND FINDING SOLUTIONS   The operator used handtools to cut the wire and twist it around the bundle. The company recognised that this task posed a risk of upper limb injury because of:

- the gripping force on the wire clippers needed to cut the wire;
- the repetitive movement of the forearm while gripping the pliers to twist the wire around the bundle.

The risks were reduced by supplying the wire ties pre-cut to the proper length and buying a new tool to twist the wires together.

The new tool was similar to a screwdriver with two grooves running down the length of the shaft. The user hooked the end of the tool in a pre-formed loop in the tie wire and pulled the tool backwards. This automatically twisted the tie with one pull. Three of the new tools were bought at about £20 each.

RESULTS   The new job design removed the wire cutting and the repetitive arm twisting movements. The operators no longer report any discomfort associated with this job.

As well as reducing risks, the redesigned task can be done faster than before. The time taken to twist a tie was reduced from 8-10 seconds to 2 seconds.

GAS COOKER 'SPLASHBACK' ASSEMBLY

TASK   The 'splashback' unit on a gas cooker is the panel behind the gas rings which prevents pans from spattering food behind the cooker. In production up to 30 rivets had to be put into each splashback unit manually using a hand-held pistol grip air gun.

PROBLEM   The operators who did this task on a regular basis were beginning to suffer from discomfort in their elbows and upper arms.

ASSESSING THE RISKS AND FINDING SOLUTIONS   The rivets were put into place with the unit lying flat on the workbench. To hold the gun at the right angle, the operator had to adopt awkward upper arm and wrist positions. The occupational health nurse for the site wanted to minimise the awkward postures.

The company provided counterbalances for the guns, and designed an adjustable rig so that the splashback unit could be held at a comfortable angle for any operator to use. The number of rivets has been halved by replacing them with projection welds.

Before

RESULTS

- Much less manual force is required to complete the operation and operators report that it is much more comfortable.
- The risk of injury has been greatly reduced.
- The quality of the finished product has been maintained.
- There are fewer trip hazards as the air hoses to the guns are now routed overhead using the counterbalancing track.
- The cost of providing the counterbalances and adjustable rigs was outweighed considerably by the savings produced using the projection welds.

After

Elbow
Upper arm

Awkward posture

Component design
Tool design
Workstation design

RIVETING OPERATIONS ARE COMMON IN LIGHT ENGINEERING INDUSTRIES. USING HAND-HELD PISTOL-GRIP GUNS ON A HORIZONTAL SURFACE FORCES THE OPERATOR INTO AWKWARD, FATIGUING, UPPER ARM POSTURES. PROVIDING ADJUSTABLE RIGS AND SUPPORTING THE WEIGHT OF THE GUNS WITH COUNTERBALANCES IS THE BEST WAY OF GETTING RID OF THESE AWKWARD POSITIONS. NEW EQUIPMENT OR COMPONENTS INTRODUCED TO INCREASE COMFORT, HEALTH, SAFETY AND PRODUCTIVITY MAY BE CHEAPER THAN THAT CURRENTLY IN USE.

COMPONENT SUB-ASSEMBLY OPERATION

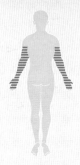

Upper limb

Grip
Applied force
Awkward posture

Component design
Task design
Workstation design

SEVERAL RISK REDUCTION PRINCIPLES WERE APPLIED TO THIS ASSEMBLY OPERATION. USING DISPENSERS FOR SCREWS AND OTHER SMALL PARTS CAN OFTEN REMOVE THE AWKWARD, PRECISE AND DIFFICULT MOVEMENTS NEEDED TO MOUNT THE COMPONENT ONTO A TOOL.

TASK The assembly line for the manufacture of franking machines had a central assembly line with 'feeder' lines supplying sub-assembled components. The main sub-tasks involved in building the machine's inter-poser (an internal component unique to such machines) included:

- putting on the bar code;
- picking up the main bracket and putting it in the jig;
- building up the main sub-component;
- putting the wires onto the main sub-component;
- putting the cir-clips in place;
- putting the springs in place;
- gluing the final component.

There were 14 separate components that made up the inter-posers which were assembled at a rate of 28 per hour. Tweezers, cir-clip applicators and a suspended powered screwdriver were used.

PROBLEM Operators had aches and pains, and upper limb disorders had been reported. There was also more than usual absenteeism, and one worker was off work for four weeks.

ASSESSING THE RISKS AND FINDING SOLUTIONS A number of risks were identified, including:

Poor grip:

- the small size of the components meant the workers had to use a pinch grip to hold, manipulate and build the inter-poser. The last three stages used the hand as a clamp to hold the inter-poser steady, while putting on the components;
- a cir-clip dispenser was used which allowed workers to pick up a cir-clip using the applicator. But, the dispensers weren't replaced often enough so the clips had to be mounted into the applicator by hand - a fiddly job;
- the glue was hard to apply, and a lot of force and a pinching grip were needed;

Poor wrist posture:

- both wrists were bent back most of the time. The right wrist was forced this way as the hand grabbed the components and put them onto the jig. Having the jig facing the workers made this worse;
- only one of the two workstations had an automatic screw dispenser.

Poor seating position:

- the workers were sitting too low at the workstation, causing more bad postures, such as raised elbows and bending the wrist towards the thumb.

The solutions involved:

- redesigning the inter-poser so that the nuts are already sunk into the plastic body. This reduced the number of assembly stages, and some of the gripping;
- putting cir-clip dispensers at both workstations, which made the cir-clips easier to apply with less force. The dispensers are replaced when empty;
- introducing soft squeeze glue bottles to remove hard pinching;

- trimming the edges of the plastic tote boxes holding the parts, making it easier to grasp the parts;
- using screw dispensers at both workstations to cut down the number of times the hand reached out, so the workers kept their hands in a better, straighter position;
- introducing high-backed height-adjustable chairs and adjustable footrests, which again improved posture and helped reduce aches and pains;
- taking regular breaks throughout the shift and introducing greater job rotation to include less hand-intensive tasks.

RESULTS A 100% reduction in reports of upper limb disorders and worker absenteeism.

LEGAL SECRETARIAL WORK

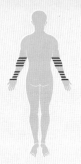

Wrist
Elbow

Repetition
Awkward posture

Individual organisation

MANY COMPANIES EMPLOY STAFF TO DO HIGHLY INTENSIVE VDU WORK TO TIGHT DEADLINES. IT IS IMPORTANT TO LOOK BEYOND THE HARDWARE TO THE DESIGN OF TASKS AND WORK ORGANISATION TO HELP TO AVOID PROBLEMS. GOOD JOB DESIGN CAN OFTEN PREVENT OR SOLVE PROBLEMS, WITHOUT NECESSARILY REQUIRING NEW EQUIPMENT TO BE BOUGHT.

TASK The work of a legal secretary in a busy firm of solicitors involved audio typing agreements, letters and legal documents to tight deadlines. On average, between 80 and 95% of the secretary's work is done on a VDU.

PROBLEM The secretary developed shooting pains in her wrists and elbows in January 1993. She reported this to the personnel department who sent her to a medical consultant who diagnosed tendonitis. She had two weeks off work, with physiotherapy, and then returned to full-time work. The problems recurred, and she stopped work again. At this point new equipment was bought for the workstation, and the company sought help from an ergonomist.

ASSESSING THE RISKS AND FINDING SOLUTIONS At the time of the ergonomist's assessment a new fully adjustable chair and a wrist-rest had been bought which made the equipment at the workstation acceptable. But each time the user returned to this job, even for short periods, the problems came back. In the ergonomist's view, the main risk factors were the lack of natural breaks in the VDU work, and the pressure of demanding deadlines.

Several weeks later a different job came up in the firm's administration unit. In August the user returned to work in this new job full time. The new workstation and equipment were almost identical to her old one, but the nature of the job changed a lot. Audio typing is still done, but only for 20-30% of the user's time. There are fewer deadlines, and the work of the unit as a whole is much less stressful.

The employer took steps to remind all secretarial and fee-earning staff about the importance of taking regular, frequent breaks from intensive keying. Although staff had been trained in the use of their workstations, breaks were believed to be so important because of the nature of the tasks, that additional written reminders were sent to staff, and further ergonomics training is planned.

The costs to the company for new equipment, medical costs, the ergonomist, sickness absence and a temporary legal secretary came to about £12 000.

RESULTS Since moving to her new job, the user is much more comfortable. Her symptoms have decreased considerably, and she estimates that she is 90% cured.

MANUFACTURING JEANS

TASK A manufacturing company produced jeans at three sites. Work involved repetitive use of sewing machines, cutting devices and other manufacturing, finishing and packaging tasks. The company had performance-related pay schemes at all three sites.

PROBLEM In 1988/89 the company got a number of compensation claims for work-related upper limb disorders. Five of the claims were backed by medical evidence, and supported by the trade union.

ASSESSING THE RISKS AND FINDING SOLUTIONS The Safety Department investigated the cases and sought advice on how to improve the workplace layout, the design of tools and machinery to prevent further cases.

It was found that all five cases had happened after staff had returned to work after absence. A Graduated Return to Work (GRTW) scheme was introduced for workers who had had a certified absence of five days or more. They returned to work at reduced productivity but were still paid average earnings. Over a number of weeks their productivity rate was gradually increased. When they reached the end of the scheme and were fully used to their job again, they returned to full productivity. Employees on the scheme were seen regularly by the company doctor to check they had no aches or pains. Individual plans were set for each employee and were reviewed when they finished. If employees still had pain, they were referred to the company doctor to review the situation.

The reporting and recording procedures were standardised and improved to keep clear and complete records of staff with symptoms. Supervisors were instructed to treat all reports of upper limbs aches and pains seriously and sympathetically. The Human Relations Manager interviewed all employees reporting symptoms (not just those who had been absent) in order to identify any possible causes. Where appropriate, employees were referred to the company doctor for treatment and advice, and specialist medical opinion if necessary. If necessary, the employee's task or workstation was studied further by the Safety Manager and the Plant Ergonomics Team to see if any ergonomic improvements were necessary.

There were a number of other options to reduce or relieve problems, including offering workers a short period of 'reduced efficiency' under the performance-related pay scheme. The measures were tailored to the individual and their condition and the results were monitored carefully.

In addition to the GRTW scheme, all employees had training in 'conditioning movements'. These are movements designed to condition the muscles and make them more flexible. They were drawn up by a physiotherapist who made regular visits to give advice and reinforce the training. For several days after holiday periods all employees had a number of extra ten minute breaks to carry out these movements, with no loss of pay. To make sure staff didn't overdo things on return, no overtime could be worked on days when they had the extra breaks. Changes were made to some of the production methods, operational procedures, and workstation designs.

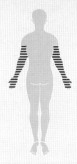

Upper limb

Repetition
Applied force

Individual organisation
Workstation design

WHERE REPETITIVE WORK CAN'T BE AVOIDED, CHANGES TO WORK ORGANISATION, COMBINED WITH WORKSTATION REDESIGN, CAN HELP REDUCE MUSCULOSKELETAL PROBLEMS. EFFECTIVE MONITORING OF STAFF AT RISK, GOOD REPORTING PROCEDURES, AND GRADUALLY BRINGING WORKERS UP TO A FULL PRODUCTION SCHEDULE CAN SIGNIFICANTLY REDUCE PROBLEMS. THESE POINTS APPLY EQUALLY TO LARGE AND SMALL OPERATIONS.

RESULTS Plant managers believed that the GRTW scheme did not reduce production. The trade unions involved were in favour of the scheme and most employees liked it. Since the changes, there have been very few compensation claims and none related to a return to work after prolonged absence. This has reduced medical and legal costs, the cost of further claims, and may also reduce insurance premiums.

ACTUATOR REMANUFACTURING

TASK When components of heavy vehicles, such as actuators, single/twin cylinder compressors, and valves are replaced as part of a vehicle's service, the 'used' components return to the plant for reconditioning and rebuilding. The used actuators have to be taken to pieces. This is a safety-critical task, because the strength of the spring in the actuator can cause the actuator to explode apart. For this reason, the actuators are taken apart in a cage (the actuator stripping rig) to contain any explosion. The rig has a counterweighted door which must be closed before the actuator is pulled apart. For this door to close positively it has to be heavier than the counterweights.

PROBLEM Staff on this operation were complaining of shoulder pain.

ASSESSING THE RISKS AND FINDING SOLUTIONS Their pain was likely to be caused by the weight of the door and the frequency with which it had to be opened and closed (up to 60 times an hour).

Before

The company fitted pneumatic cylinders to the three stripping rigs to operate the door automatically. Instead of manually lifting the door up and down, the operator pushes two buttons to raise and lower it. The total cost of modifying all three rigs was £4430.

RESULTS

- The manual force needed to do this job is much reduced and there is no more risk of injury and discomfort to the shoulder and upper arms.
- The task is easier and less fatigue has meant that more actuators can be stripped per day.
- The risk of trapping fingers under the door has been removed.

Shoulder

*Applied force
Repetition*

Machinery design

MANY LIGHT AND HEAVY ENGINEERING INDUSTRIES USE FIXED AND/OR INTERLOCKING GUARDS TO PROTECT OPERATORS FROM HARM FROM EXPLOSION, SPINNING COMPONENTS, BLADES ETC. SUCH GUARDS ARE SAFE BUT CAN BE VERY TIRING FOR OPERATORS IF HEAVY AND UNWIELDY DOORS HAVE TO BE OPENED AND CLOSED. THIS PART OF THE TASK CAN OFTEN BE AUTOMATED QUITE EASILY, REDUCING UPPER LIMB DISCOMFORT AND OPERATOR FATIGUE.

COIL HANDLING

Back
Shoulder

Applied force
Awkward posture

Machinery design

Before   *After*

TASK Operators in a luggage manufacturing plant manoeuvred a large drum of steel wire into a machine for winding the wire into coil springs. About four times each shift the operators removed the empty drum and replaced it with a new one weighing 365 kg.

PROBLEM One serious back injury had occurred, and there were reports of back and shoulder pain.

ASSESSING THE RISKS AND FINDING SOLUTIONS Because of the heavy weight of the drum manoeuvring it took a lot of effort from the operator's back and shoulders. Although rolling the drum was relatively easy, a lot of pushing and pulling was needed to turn it and line it up with the feeder on the machine. This put large stresses on the operator's back and shoulders. The low height of the drum also meant the operator was pushing in a stooped position, again increasing the risk of injury.

A modified wheelbarrow handle was used to steer and roll the drum with far less effort. A wheelbarrow handle was attached to a piece of steel tubing inserted into the centre of the drum to act as an axle. The handle gave the operators greater leverage when turning the drum, and allowed them to work in a more upright position. The handle was made in-house for about £20.

RESULTS The handle greatly reduced the effort the operators had to use to fit the drums of wire. They used the handle by choice, and there have been no reports of back or shoulder pains or any injuries since.

BATTERY REPLACEMENT ON AUTOMATIC GUIDED VEHICLES

TASK With the installation of a new Automatic Guided Vehicle (AGV) system, operatives had to replace batteries in AGVs as they were required.

PROBLEM The batteries were heavy and would need at least two operatives to move them manually.

ASSESSING THE RISKS AND FINDING SOLUTIONS It was clear that the operatives risked serious back injuries because of the weight and the way they had to carry the batteries, and injuries to their legs and feet if they dropped them.

Purpose-built battery racks and trolleys were designed in-house. The trolleys and racks were built at the same height as the AGV, so the batteries could be moved at one level from the rack to the trolley, and from the trolley onto the AGV. To make sure the trolley and rack were in line and held still when the batteries were moved, the trolleys were fitted with pegs which fitted into holes in the racking system. Handles were fitted to the batteries to help pull them into place.

The racks and trolleys were fitted with rollers so that the battery could be removed and replaced from one to the other. A catch was fitted to the trolley to stop the battery moving about while it was being transported.

The system was designed quickly and cost effectively by staff in-house. The only viable alternative would have been to install a cumbersome and expensive crane lift.

Back

Manual handling

Mechanisation

After

TROLLEY AND RACKING SYSTEMS CAN MAKE STORING AND TRANSPORTING MANY LARGE, HEAVY OR HAZARDOUS GOODS MUCH EASIER. IT IS IMPORTANT TO MAKE SURE THAT COMPONENT PARTS ARE COMPATIBLE, EG BY MAKING THE SURFACES THE SAME LEVEL.

RESULTS
- Risk of manual handling injuries reduced.
- Batteries can be fitted more quickly.
- Increased flexibility of staff, allowing them to do other tasks.

UPENDING WHISKY CASKS

Back

Manual handling
Awkward posture

Mechanisation

TASK Whisky casks, normally stored on their sides, sometimes need upending - for example to repair a leak, or to transport. Casks were upended traditionally using the brute force of three people. With one man at one end of the cask and two on each side, the cask was rocked until with one large push it stood on its end. Each cask held 110 gallons and weighed 500 kg.

PROBLEM Several cask handlers had been injured doing this. There was a risk of back injuries and that the cask could slip and fall towards them, particularly if the floor was wet and slippery.

ASSESSING THE PROBLEM AND FINDING SOLUTIONS The job was risky because it needed a low, stooped posture to hold the cask, and a large pushing and lifting force. The men at the sides also twisted their bodies awkwardly as they worked.

A portable cask upender costing £3000 was developed. It allowed one person, with mechanical assistance, to upend the cask. Straps with hinges at either side were put around the middle of the cask and the hinges connected to couplings on the upender. A lever was then lightly pumped to raise the arm of the upender. With the cask suspended it could easily be turned upright. The arm was lowered until the cask was standing on the ground. The physical effort needed by the operators was greatly reduced.

AN OLD, TRADITIONAL METHOD OF CARRYING OUT A TASK WAS LOOKED AT AFRESH. IN THIS CASE A MECHANICAL AID REDUCED THE RISK OF BACK INJURIES. UPENDING OR INVERTING MACHINES ARE ALSO BECOMING MORE COMMON IN THE CHEMICAL INDUSTRY FOR HANDLING LARGE DRUMS.

Before

After

RESULTS Since introducing the upender, reports of back pain have fallen. The risk of casks slipping and falling has been completely removed.

The cask upender has been introduced in several distilleries and warehouses, and has been especially successful in small sites where having few staff made it hard to use the traditional upending method, or meant drawing vital staff away from other areas of the operation.

STILLAGING CASK BEER

TASK One of the most physically demanding and common handling tasks in the brewing industry is 'stillaging' (or 'thrawling') casks of beer in retail outlets, eg pubs. Real ale must be put on a stillage (a low platform or bench) before being served, and not moved once it has been tapped. This allows the sediments from fermentation in the cask to settle. In the traditional stillaging method a drayman or public house worker:

- manoeuvres a cask to the edge of the stillage;
- lifts one end of the cask which rests on the edge of the stillage;
- pushes the barrel back until the corner of the stillage is near the middle of the cask;
- lifts and pushes the lower end of the cask onto the stillage;
- pushes the cask into place on the stillage;
- secures the stillage with wedges.

Before

After

PROBLEM When stillaging casks, pub or brewery workers are stooped over and lifting heavy weights. There is a high risk of manual handling injury. The areas where stillaging usually takes place, such as pub cellars, are often cramped, dark and slippery. These conditions increase the risks. Stillaging is one of the most dangerous handling tasks in the brewing industry.

ASSESSING THE RISKS AND FINDING SOLUTIONS The risk of manual handling injury comes from the lifting and pushing actions described above.

A large national brewery adopted a new gantry which allows a person to stillage a cask by rolling it back on a sled-like device. It was developed with a small engineering firm specialising in equipment for the brewing industry.

The gantry has a pair of curved bars running along one end. It is clipped securely onto the side of the cask, with its curved side on the bottom. The cask is then rolled back into place on this curved end, lifting the bottom end up until the cask is on its side, ready to be tapped. Each gantry cost about £40.

RESULTS The new gantry changes the nature of the handling task:

- draymen can push the cask forward in a controlled manner instead of having to lift and push at the same time on the edge of a slippery stillage;
- it allows a more upright posture and needs less physical force;
- the curved front of the gantry allows the cask to be tilted forward when nearly empty so more of the beer can be served;
- feedback from pub staff and draymen is very positive;
- the job is easier, and it is easier to train new staff.

Back

Manual handling Awkward posture

Mechanisation

THE GANTRY MAY BE APPLIED TO ANY STILLAGING OPERATIONS. THE SAME TYPE OF DEVICE CAN BE USED FOR HANDLING OTHER LARGE BARRELS, SUCH AS OIL DRUMS, WHICH MAY HAVE TO BE STORED ON THEIR SIDES.

FITTING SEATS INTO VEHICLES

Back

Manual handling
Awkward posture
Repetition

Mechanisation

MODIFICATIONS TO WORKSTATIONS TO IMPROVE HEALTH AND SAFETY CAN OFTEN LEAD TO PRODUCTION BENEFITS AS WELL.

TASK Driver and passenger seats are fitted into vans in the last stages of the production process. The seats are lifted off a conveyor, or out of a delivery crate, manoeuvred into the front or rear of the van by two operators, and bolted to the floor. The operators fitted about twelve seats an hour.

PROBLEM The seats weigh up to 38 kg. The task was associated with a risk of back injury.

ASSESSING THE RISKS AND FINDING SOLUTIONS The site health and safety manager assessed the task, and made it a high priority for action because of the risk from heavy, awkward and repetitive lifting. He wanted to remove the need for manual lifting altogether.

Three counterbalanced hoists, costing £5000 each, were purchased for each of the fitting areas.

RESULTS

- The risk of back injury has been reduced with all of the weight taken by the hoist, not the operators.
- Operators experience much less fatigue, and prefer using the hoist.
- The task can now be carried out by one operator.
- There is no more scratch damage to the floor of the vehicle, which was common when the operators lifted the seats into position.
- The time taken to complete the task has been reduced.

REMANUFACTURE COMPONENT SORTING

TASK When components from heavy vehicles (eg actuators, single/twin cylinder compressors, valves) are replaced as part of a vehicle's service, the 'used' components return to the plant for reconditioning and rebuilding. The used equipment returns from the service companies in crates, unsorted. In the remanufacturing plant it has to be sorted into other crates by hand before being stripped down for remanufacture.

PROBLEM This task was seen as posing a risk of injury to operators' shoulders and backs because of manually handling the heavy equipment.

ASSESSING THE RISKS AND FINDING SOLUTIONS It was difficult for operators to pick up the components correctly, because of the high sides of the delivery crates. They had to lean into the crates and stretch to pick up the components at the bottom.

The company purchased a handling trolley with powered lift and tilt mechanisms. Using this, the crates of unsorted components are raised to a comfortable height for the operator, and tilted towards them so that they do not need to lean and stretch to get to any of the components. The trolley cost £2300.

Before

After

RESULTS

- Operators report that the task is easier, as there is much less stretching and consequently less fatigue at the end of the working day.
- The risk of shoulder and back injury from this operation has been removed.
- The task takes slightly longer to perform using the trolley but operators much prefer it.

*Back
Shoulder*

*Manual handling
Awkward posture*

Mechanisation

WHERE THE NEED TO LIFT HEAVY COMPONENTS CANNOT EASILY BE AVOIDED, THE TASK CAN BE MADE AS COMFORTABLE AS POSSIBLE FOR OPERATORS BY PROVIDING A MECHANICAL DEVICE TO PLACE THE COMPONENTS AT THE BEST HEIGHT AND POSITION. LIFTING TROLLEYS CAN MINIMISE THE DISTANCE THE OPERATOR HAS TO CARRY A LOAD, AND REMOVE THE NEED FOR AWKWARD BENDING AND STRETCHING.

PREPARATION, WEIGHING AND MIXING OF RAW MATERIALS

Back

*Manual handling
Repetition*

*Mechanisation
Workstation design*

MANUAL HANDLING OF RAW MATERIALS IS COMMON IN SEVERAL INDUSTRIES, ESPECIALLY THE FOOD AND CHEMICAL INDUSTRIES. VACUUM LIFTING DEVICES CAN TAKE AWAY MOST OF THE PHYSICAL EFFORT NEEDED TO LIFT HEAVY LOADS. ALSO, ALWAYS LOOK FOR WAYS TO REDUCE THE NUMBER OF TIMES THE SAME LOAD IS HANDLED.

TASK   Operators at a medical supplies company handled 50 kg sacks of raw materials, in four stages, to make up a mixture. They:

- lifted the bags from the supplier's pallet to the transfer pallet, turning them to tear off the outer layer of packaging paper, and re-labelled them with a stamp;
- lifted the bags on to a one metre high scale to measure the weight;
- lifted the bags from the scale back to the pallet;
- lifted the bags, cut them open and emptied the contents into a two metre high mixer. This involved two people.

Two operators were preparing between 16 000 kg and 21 000 kg of raw materials each week. Because each sack was handled several times, each operator was handling 28 000 kg to 35 000 kg in a week.

PROBLEM   60% of the operators had reported back pain, and two had suffered acute back injuries. The back pain led to several periods of employee absenteeism, including three instances where the employee was off work for over four weeks. Because of production needs, the amount handled was due to increase.

ASSESSING THE RISKS AND FINDING SOLUTIONS

Hazard/risk	*Solution*
Large batch sizes with heavy loads.	Handling done by operators on all three shifts rather than one shift only - spreading the load. A third of the raw material was supplied in 25 kg instead of 50 kg packages - making it easier to handle.
Each load handled several times.	Handling was removed in three of the four stages by: - installing a vacuum hoist, costing £7300, to transfer bags from the supplier's pallet. This also made removing the packaging easy while the bag was suspended; - introducing a floor level scale, costing £4000, to allow several bags to be weighed at the same time, with the operator using a pallet handler to move the pallets.
Loads transferred to and from very low and high levels.	This was solved in some stages by the equipment introduced above. The company are considering a vacuum hoist to help put the raw materials into the mixer.

Before   *After*

RESULTS   The raw materials are now handled more quickly. Throughput has
increased between 80% and 100% with the same number of staff. No back pain has
been reported in the two and a half years the system has been installed, even among
staff who had reported symptoms before.

GAS COOKER ASSEMBLY

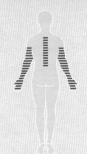

Back
Upper limb

Manual handling
Awkward posture

Mechanisation
Tool design
Workstation design

IN MANY INDUSTRIES, OPERATORS HAVE TO MANOEUVRE PRODUCTS AND USE TOOLS AT AWKWARD ANGLES TO PUT FINISHING TOUCHES TO PRODUCTS. PROVIDING SIMPLE MECHANICAL AIDS SUCH AS TURNTABLES TO REMOVE THE NEED FOR HANDLING IS OFTEN THE BEST WAY OF REDUCING THE RISKS FROM LIFTING AND STRETCHING.

TASK   In the final stages of gas cooker manufacture, the cookers have to be manoeuvred into different positions to apply the finishing touches - the last rivets on the top, back and sides, and the test cycle equipment. The gas cookers arrived on roller tracks and had to be manually manoeuvred into the correct positions for riveting etc. Rivets were applied with hand-held pistol-grip air guns.

PROBLEM   There was a risk of upper limb and back injury from manual handling of the cookers, and from awkward reaching with heavy tools.

Before

After

ASSESSING THE RISKS AND FINDING SOLUTIONS

Hazard/risk	*Solution*
Manual turning and tilting of cookers.	Turntables provided to eliminate manual handling.
Reaching inside and around the cooker holding heavy air guns. Trip hazards from airgun hoses.	Counter-balances fitted to guns to take their weight and route hoses out of the way.
Awkward reaches because of the roller tracks - operators had to follow cookers at busy times.	Sections of the track can be disconnected so that operators don't have to run after cookers dragging hoses and guns.

The cost of equipping the line was £30 000.

RESULTS   Using this new equipment, the need to lift and turn the cookers is reduced. It is now much easier to position the appropriate surface of the cooker comfortably for the operator to work on. The benefits of the new system include:

- the need for stretching and twisting has been totally removed;
- the risk of back injury has been removed;
- the operation is easier to manage, as anyone can now do the work - previously it was restricted to strong, fit men;
- the job is more comfortable and less fatiguing;
- there are fewer trip hazards in the workplace;
- the time needed to carry out the tasks has reduced, and productivity has improved;
- there is less chance of damaging the product (eg chipping the enamel) with the air guns as they are lighter and easier to manoeuvre;
- there is less stress associated with the task as operators can stop the track when they need to, to work on a particular cooker.

Although reducing the risk of injury was the driving force behind the new track, the considerable productivity and quality benefits will soon compensate for the costs.

RECOVERY OF SHOPPING TROLLEYS FROM CAR PARKS

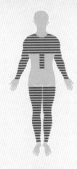

Back
Shoulder
Upper and lower limb

Applied force
Awkward posture
Manual handling

Mechanisation

SIMILAR SOLUTIONS CAN BE SUCCESSFUL IN A RANGE OF TASKS. ADAPTING AN EXISTING UNIT TO HELP HANDLE SIMILAR UNITS COULD BE USED, FOR EXAMPLE IN PRODUCTION PLANTS WHERE MOVING TUBS OF COMPONENTS IS COMMON.

TASK   Staff had to retrieve shopping trolleys from supermarket car parks where they had been left by shoppers. In larger stores a powered vehicle was used but in smaller stores this was not cost-effective. Instead the task was done manually by an operative linking up to 15 trolleys to form a long 'snake' (which reduced the number of trips made).

PROBLEM   A number of operatives had suffered strained muscles and soft tissue injuries while trying to manoeuvre and control these 'snakes'. It was important that staff kept control of the trolleys because of the damage to pedestrians or vehicles that could occur if they got out of control.

ASSESSING THE RISKS AND FINDING SOLUTIONS   The main risks came from having to continually keep control of the line of trolleys, sometimes on uneven or sloping surfaces. Staff had to push hard to make the trolleys go the right way while stooping over them. A design consultant was brought in to work with the company to identify the requirements for a solution to the trolley recovery task. These included ease of use, maintainability, purchase and running costs, safety, level of training, handling characteristics, and numbers of trolleys to be 'driven'.

A standard trolley chassis fitted with a rechargeable electric power unit was developed. This would be used to 'drive' the line of trolleys. Prototypes were trialled at different supermarkets to give information on a range of situations, and to maximise staff consultation. The design took on board the staff's suggestions. Reactions and the benefits achieved were monitored informally.

Before

After

RESULTS   Feedback from the staff consultation was positive. The effort needed and awkward postures were reduced. The number of recovery journeys reduced by 42.5%. The simple controls involved minimal staff training.

The new trolley cost £10 000 to develop, with an initial set-up cost per supermarket of about £6000. This was believed to be acceptable, weighed against the benefits of reduced injuries and sickness leave, and increased recovery efficiency.

DECANTING PARTS FOR CAR ASSEMBLY

Before

After

Upper limb

*Repetiition
Applied force*

Mechanisation

TASK At a car manufacturing plant operators had to load loose brackets and clips into feed chutes, for later use in assembly at the workstation. The operator filled the chutes by repeatedly grabbing handfuls of parts from the storage boxes below the chutes and dropping them into the chutes.

PROBLEM The task of filling the feed chutes by hand caused fatigue and presented a risk of injury to the upper limbs over time. There were also cases of employees cutting their hands on the metal parts which caught into their gloves. All operators complained about these risks.

ASSESSING THE RISKS AND FINDING SOLUTIONS The repetitiveness and gripping forces required increased the risk of upper limb disorders. A new decanting system was designed involving a small hopper which can be moved in front of the feeder chutes and contents poured into the chute.

The materials for the change cost £100.

RESULTS The decanting system reduces the repetitiveness of the task and removes the need to grasp the parts by hand. Operators can also fill the chutes more quickly. They find the new system easier to work with and less fatiguing. The change also improved housekeeping as parts do not fall on the floor. It saves on the cost of lost or damaged parts, and improves efficiency.

PARTS BINS ARE FILLED IN MOST ASSEMBLY AND MANUFACTURING INDUSTRIES. SIMPLE INNOVATIONS, LIKE SMALL HOPPERS, CAN IMPROVE SAFETY AND EFFICIENCY.

FOLDING AND STITCHING MATERIAL

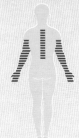

Upper limb
Back

Awkward posture
Applied force
Repetition

Mechanisation
Individual organisation

HIGHLY REPETITIVE OPERATIONS CAN BE COST-EFFECTIVELY AUTOMATED. AUTOMATION OR SEMI-AUTOMATION OF SOME COMPLEX TASKS MAY LEAD TO AN INCREASE IN PRODUCTIVITY AS WELL AS REMOVING HARMFUL POSTURES AND FORCEFUL AND REPETITIVE ACTIONS. BUT, IT IS ESSENTIAL THAT AUTOMATION DOES NOT INTRODUCE OTHER NEW POSTURES WHICH ARE HARMFUL TO THE WORKER.

TASK When jeans are manufactured a piece of material needs to be sewn into the partially made jeans above the back pocket. To ensure the materials are securely fastened together the two pieces are folded over each other to form a strong, s-shaped bond.

PROBLEM The company realised that this task presented a risk of upper limb disorders, and there had been some complaints from staff.

ASSESSING THE RISKS AND FINDING SOLUTIONS Three main problems were identified:

- The two pieces of material had to be aligned as they were stitched together. Employees often pulled back one of the pieces halfway through the process to make sure they would be in line when they had finished, putting strain on their wrists.
- Forceful and repetitive finger movements were needed to hold and align the material as it was stitched together.
- The jeans were supplied to the employees in bundles stacked on trolleys. From a sitting position they stretched upwards to reach the highest pair of jeans, and then bent down to reach the last pair on the trolley. This frequent handling in awkward postures created a risk of back injury.

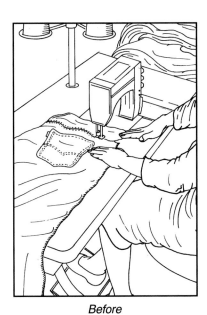

Before

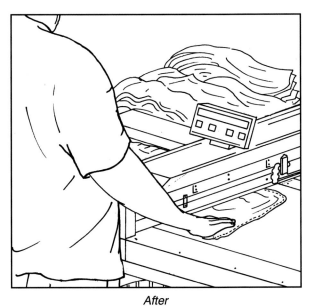

After

The company's Research and Development Team designed a machine to automatically sew the two pieces of material together. The employee fed in the material, and the machine automatically aligned them, folded them over and stitched them together before stacking them on a trolley for removal. Employees could set the pace of their work themselves.

To remove the handling problem, the jeans were supplied on an automatic hoist which raised itself so the jeans were presented at the right height to reach comfortably. Hoists were introduced throughout the plant.

The Company's engineering department were keen to introduce the machine, and the reduction in risk that it would bring was a major factor in the case for capital investment.

RESULTS   The risk of musculoskeletal injury was greatly reduced as the harmful finger and wrist movements were removed, and the postures associated with handling the jeans greatly improved.

Both product and process quality improved. The automated machinery produced the garments more uniformly and with higher quality. The machine-produced jeans were more evenly stacked and so less likely to fall off the trolley. Productivity also increased by 20% to 30% with no increase in staff.

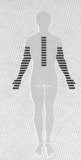

Back
Upper limb

Awkward posture

Automation

COMPUTER-CONTROLLED MECHANICAL LIFTING DEVICES CAN HELP REDUCE MANUAL HANDLING PROBLEMS IN ANY PRODUCTION LINE PROCESS WHERE THE COMPONENT IS LARGE OR HEAVY.

TASK   Operators had to work on heavy engines moving along a production line, adding various components to them as they were transported around the factory on a conveyor belt.

PROBLEM   Each engine was too large to be lifted manually, so the operators had to stand and work on it in whatever position it was in when it reached them. This meant they had to work in awkward postures to reach the different areas they had to work on - stooping, bending, twisting, and reaching away from the body.

A new product range was to be introduced. Management decided that with careful design and staff consultation they could reduce or remove the musculoskeletal problems.

ASSESSING THE RISKS AND FINDING SOLUTIONS Consultation with staff, different departments, and suppliers led to a major reorganisation of the plant and production process.

To remove the need for operators to work in awkward positions they introduced computer-controlled pallets and automatically guided vehicles (AGVs) to manoeuvre the engines. The design of the pallets allowed the engines to rest in the right positions for the operators to work on them comfortably. The engines are automatically lifted at points around the line and put down in the right position for the next stage in the process.

RESULTS
- Musculoskeletal injuries reduced by 91%.
- Productivity increased by 49%.
- Product quality improved.
- Staff flexibility increased.

TASK Operators in an assembly plant used a manual drilling machine to ream holes in metal caps which form part of the starter for an outboard marine motor. The operator took the part from the boxes behind her, placed them on the machine and manually pulled down the lever with her right hand.

Before

PROBLEM There were some complaints of shoulder discomfort, and a risk of cumulative injury to the upper limb and back. No injuries had been reported.

ASSESSING THE RISKS AND FINDING SOLUTIONS With the lever overhead, the operator had to bend and twist at the same time as exerting overhead force to pull it down.

The ergonomics team studying the job realised that a similar operation was being performed nearby using a Jarvis Multi-spindle automatic drill/tap.

The company moved the operation from the manual drilling machine to the Jarvis machine. The automated operation removed the awkward postures and pulling. Because the machinery was already on site, there was no additional cost.

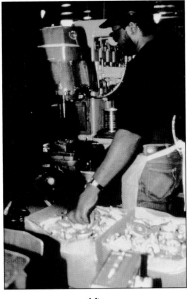

After

RESULTS This new method resulted in a 22% increase in production, which translated into £1.60 labour savings per 100 units, or almost £650 annual savings.

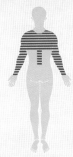

Upper limb
Back
Shoulder

Awkward posture
Applied force

Automation

MANUAL DRILLING MACHINES ARE COMMON THROUGHOUT MANUFACTURING AND FABRICATION TYPE INDUSTRIES. MODERN TECHNOLOGY, WHICH MAY ALREADY EXIST IN-HOUSE, CAN OFTEN REDUCE THE RISK OF ERGONOMICS-RELATED INJURIES AS WELL AS PROVIDE PRODUCTIVITY BENEFITS.

SEWING HEMS ON JEANS

Wrist

*Applied force
Repetition
Awkward posture*

Automation

CONSTANT EXERTION OF PRESSURE CAN LEAD TO HARMFUL STRAIN ON THE MUSCLES. USE OF MACHINERY OR MECHANICAL AIDS CAN REMOVE THIS RISK AND CAN LEAD TO MORE CONSISTENT QUALITY IN PRODUCT MANUFACTURE.

TASK Jeans have a hem sewn into the bottom of the legs to strengthen the border. Workers folded over the material a number of times and sewed it together using a sewing machine. This was done for a large part of the day.

PROBLEM One worker was moved to another task because of pains in her wrists. Many of the workers who sewed hems regularly wore wrist straps to support their wrists.

ASSESSING THE RISKS AND FINDING SOLUTIONS Folding over the denim before sewing needed a lot of effort, as did holding it in place to stitch it. The force needed to complete the task, coupled with its repetitive nature, put a substantial strain on the fingers and the wrist, and was likely to be the cause of the injuries.

The company developed a machine which would take in the folded hem, hold it and turn it around and stitch it into place.

Before

After

RESULTS The harmful wrist postures and pressures were largely removed and many of the workers no longer needed to wear wrist supports.

This change led to health improvements, an increase in morale, a reduction in staff turnover and sickness absence, and ultimately a reduced likelihood of claims for compensation for musculoskeletal injury. Further cost savings were made from the reduction in staff training costs, legal and medical expenditure, and costs of hiring temporary staff. Product quality also improved.

FURTHER PUBLICATIONS AND SOURCES OF ADVICE

HSE PRICED PUBLICATIONS

Display Screen Equipment Work Guidance on Regulations
L26 1992 HSE Books ISBN 0 7176 1410 1

Management of Health and Safety at Work Approved Code of Practice
L21 1992 HSE Books ISBN 0 7176 0412 8

Manual Handling Operations Guidance on Regulations
L23 1992 HSE Books ISBN 0 7176 0411 X

Manual Handling - Solutions You Can Handle
HS(G)115 1994 HSE Books ISBN 0 7176 0693 7

Work Equipment Guidance on Regulations
L22 1993 HSE Books ISBN 0 7176 0414 4

Work Related Upper Limb Disorders - A Guide to Prevention
HS(G)60 1990 HSE Books ISBN 0 11 885565 4

VDUs: an easy guide to the Regulations
HS(G)90 1994 HSE Books ISBN 0 7176 0735 6

HSE FREE PUBLICATIONS

Getting to Grips with Manual Handling - A Short Guide for Employers
1993 IND(G)143(L)

If the Task Fits - Ergonomics At Work (rev)
1994 IND(G)90(L)

Upper Limb Disorders - Assessing the Risk
1994 IND(G)171(L)

Working with VDUs
1992 IND(G)36(L)

OTHER PUBLICATIONS

Case Studies in Ergonomics Practice Volume 2, Design for Work and Use
H G Maule and J S Weiner (eds) London: Taylor and Francis 1981
ISBN 0 85066 208 7

Ergonomics For Beginners - A Quick Reference Guide
J Dul and B Weerdmeester 10th Edition Taylor and Francis 1993 ISBN 0 74840079 6

Health, Safety and Ergonomics
A S Nicholson and J E Ridds (eds) London: Butterworths 1988 ISBN 0 408 02386 4

Increasing Productivity and Profit Through Health and Safety
M Oxenburgh North Ryde CCH International 1991 ISBN 1 86264 264 8

Kaizen Key to Japan
Masaaki Imai. McGraw Hill 1986 ISBN 0 07 554332 X

Making the Job Easier. An Ergonomic Ideas Book
National Safety Council Chicago, IL: NSC, 1988

Participatory Ergonomics
K Noro and A S Imada Taylor and Francis 1991 ISBN 0 85066382 2

TUC Guide to Assessing WRULD's Risks
Dr Peter Buckle and Joanne Hoffman, Trades Union Congress 1994
ISBN 1 85006 277 3

ADVICE FROM HEALTH AND SAFETY AUTHORITIES

For businesses in office or retail premises, contact the Environmental Health Department at your local Council.

For other premises, contact the nearest Health and Safety Executive Area Office, as listed in Yellow Pages.